A Pocket Tour™
of Money
on the Internet

Mark Fister

San Francisco ◆ Paris ◆ Düsseldorf ◆ Soest

SYBEX

Pocket Tour concept:	Brenda Kienan
Acquisitions Manager:	Kristine Plachy
Developmental Editor:	Brenda Kienan
Editor:	Doug Robert
Project Editor:	Emily Smith
Technical Editor:	Samuel Faulkner
Book Designer:	Emil Yanos
Graphic Artist:	Cuong Le
Desktop Publisher:	Molly Sharp
Proofreader/Production Assistant:	Taris Duffié
Indexer:	Ted Laux
Cover Designer:	Joanna Gladden
Cover Illustrator:	Mike Miller

Acknowledgments

I want to thank a number of people for all their support and assistance during the writing of this book. Top on the list are my wife, Patricia Fister, who picked up the slack and accommodated my many needs; my mom and dad, Judy and Lee Fister, for inspiring and encouraging me in this endeavor; and Mike Cristante, for always being there to play backgammon when I needed to relax.

At SYBEX, Doug Robert, Brenda Kienan, and Emily Smith helped me to sculpt this work into its final form. All of the people at the American Association of Individual Investors, where I spend most of my waking hours, deserve honorable mention. It is a great place to work.

And, of course, all of my friends and relatives deserve credit too. A special mention goes to Tom Allen, my advisor at MIT; his guidance and support contributed significantly to my interest in computers and overall development in school.

Table of Contents

Introduction

The Pocket Tour of Money is about investment sites on the Internet, that is, areas on the Internet that provide valuable information to people making investment planning decisions. When I began researching this book, I came across many sites listed in magazine articles and investment news publications—but in most cases there was no in-depth, detailed review of what each site offered. It is true that anyone with some investing and Internet experience can easily find these site addresses and explore the resources themselves. But two problems exist: not everyone *has* experience in investing and in using the Internet, and most people realistically don't have the time or money to investigate the many resources located at each of those sites. As I got on the Internet and explored the various sites, I realized that a person would have to spend a great deal of time to really understand what a given site has to offer, and that time online can be both expensive and futile.

I decided then that this book would aim to achieve three goals: First, you can use this book to learn how to become an informed individual investor. Second, you'll learn how to navigate through the Internet and within a given Internet site to get financial information. And third, you'll learn where to go to find Internet sites that have the information you seek.

 If you are an individual investor, or would like to start investing, this book will help you to understand the basic principles of investing and of the Internet. This book will also help new or experienced investors quickly find sites in what can be a very intimidating and sprawling space.

And please remember, this book is a pocket *tour*. I won't just say, "Here's a list of sites, go have fun." I wrote this book from the perspective of a guide; I'll be the person who takes you on a tour of the many financial and investment sites out there. I won't just hand you a map and say "see you later"— a good guide goes with you, leading and pointing out all sorts of things, both good and bad. I point out exceptional resources and potential pitfalls, where appropriate, to help save you time finding the places you should visit.

Finally, I wrote this book on my own, in my spare time. It has not been edited or approved by the organization I work for—the American Association of Individual Investors (AAII). Consequently, the views taken in this book are strictly my own (although I would be happy to think that my associates at AAII like this book). If you have any questions or comments, you can contact me at mfister@interaccess.com.

ORGANIZATION

I've arranged this book in two parts. Part One, The Basics, is for anyone who lacks background or experience with investing *or* using the Internet. If you are new to investing, make sure to read An Overview of Investing in Part One, where I explain the basic principles of financial planning and investing. I'll break all the areas down into their basics and spell everything out very clearly in case you happen to be a first-time investor—it's always a good time to start! I've even included a glossary to help with several financial and investment terms that may be unfamiliar to you. And for those of you who haven't yet hooked up to the Net—Part One is for you too. I'll cure anyone's Internet anxiety by clearly explaining what the Internet is, how to get connected, and how to actually *use* it. I will tell you what all that Internet jargon is (like Gopher, the Web, etc.) and exactly how you can use these tools to find the great stuff you've been hearing about. Whether you are a *newbie* (a beginner on the Internet) or just need a refresher, Part One was written with you in mind.

While Part One establishes the framework and gives you the knowledge to fully investigate investment resources on the Internet, Part Two is where you will find the real gems. Part Two covers specific investment sites on the Internet in great detail. I've divided Part Two into ten sections, with each section addressing a certain area within the subject of investing. Looking strictly for sites with mutual fund analysis? online trading? portfolio management? No need to spend hours on your own testing every site you see that has something to do with money. I'll take you directly to where you want to go and help you find what you're looking for. Not only do I provide addresses for all the sites discussed, but I give my own review—I'll let you know if I found the site disappointing, extremely valuable, or somewhere in between.

You'll probably want to refer to the Table of Contents to quickly locate sites you may have heard about, but otherwise, I suggest finding the investment section you're interested in in Part Two and then browsing through the sites I have listed—you may find a great one you never thought could be useful! The sites mentioned in each section appear in alphabetical order. In Part Two you'll notice that some sites appear in several sections if they provide information pertinent to more than one area of investing. QuoteCom, for example, is listed under five sections. This isn't an attempt to pad pages—what I've done is discuss the site only as it relates to the topic of each section. For example, in the Technical Analysis section I discuss QuoteCom's services that provide end-of-day price updates for securities listed on domestic exchanges, historical price data, and other resources, but *only as they relate to technical analysis*. In the section on Portfolio Management, I discuss only those of QuoteCom's services that are relevant to portfolio management—setting up a portfolio of up to 50 securities, receiving daily valuation reports, and setting upper and lower price alarms. This way, the information is where you expect to find it.

CONVENTIONS

I've made use of several features in this *Pocket Tour* to help you get the most out of your reading. The following margin icons are used liberally throughout Parts One and Two to highlight pertinent information or to point out trouble spots that you may encounter:

This icon indicates that I'm going to explain a note of additional information that you may find useful.

This icon will accompany a tip that may help you save money, save time, or navigate more efficiently on the Internet.

Pay close attention when you see this icon! Here I will warn you of pitfalls and potential trouble spots. I may also help you to avoid making mistakes or uninformed decisions.

In Part Two I've used additional icons to mark the types of addresses you'll find:

 indicates a site on the World Wide Web

 indicates a site where you can make use of a Gopher

 indicates a Telnet site

 indicates a Newsgroup

 indicates a site that requires File Transfer Protocol (FTP)

 indicates an e-mail address

 indicates a Bulletin Board System (BBS)

If you're starting to feel confused already, don't be. As I said earlier, I will explain what all of these terms mean and how to use them in Part One.

 Finally, I have designated several sites as being particularly noteworthy. These sites are marked with an *Author's Pick* icon. In selecting which sites to give this "thumbs up" rating, I based my decision on the relative quantity and quality of the information that a site provides. Not every section in Part Two has an entry with an Author's Pick. For example, the last section of Part Two deals with sites that provide trading services via the Internet. Because I did not open accounts with each of these services and thoroughly test each of them, no Author's Pick ratings are given for that section.

Part One: The Basics

An Overview of Investing

 This book has two parts. The first, this one, provides a general overview about investing and the Internet—just enough to point you in the right direction so that you can get up and running. If you are already up to speed with the terminology of finance and investing, or are already "Internet-aware," feel free to go to the main part of this book (Part Two), which covers the best and most popular areas and resources on the Internet that you can use in making your investment decisions.

I know that you are anxious to start checking out various investment resources on the Internet, but it would help if we have some sense of organization and direction as we go from one resource to the next. In this part of the book I begin by dividing the investment process into several categories:

◆ personal financial planning

◆ portfolio management

◆ fundamental stock analysis

◆ fixed-income analysis

◆ mutual fund analysis

◆ futures and options

◆ technical analysis

◆ economic analysis

For each of these categories I'll present some of the basic tenets, things you should keep in mind when evaluating the usefulness of an investment resource. After providing you with an overview of investing, I will present an overview of the Internet. This overview will cover:

◆ a brief history

◆ getting connected

◆ Internet tools

Then it's on to Part Two, where I present the most popular and useful Internet sites for the individual investor.

PERSONAL FINANCIAL PLANNING

You might be wondering, isn't financial planning too general to be included in a discussion about investing? After all, financial planning is about

◆ budgeting your finances,

◆ managing your taxes,

◆ making decisions about insurance coverage,

◆ planning for retirement, and

◆ planning your estate.

How do these concerns fit into your personal investment planning? Figure 1.1 shows the parts of financial planning as a flow chart to indicate how one part affects another.

You shouldn't consider one area without including the others. For example, consider credit card debt: when it comes to deciding where to invest your money, you are probably better off paying any outstanding credit card debt rather than investing that money in stocks or bonds. This is because most credit card companies charge interest rates over 12.5%; you would be hard pressed to realize greater after-tax gains than this from your investments on a consistent basis over time.

The following sections examine how some areas of personal financial planning relate to investing.

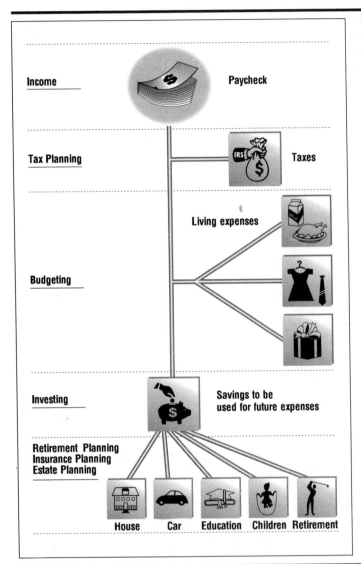

Figure 1.1:
A flow chart of the personal financial planning process

Income — Paycheck

Tax Planning — Taxes

Living expenses

Budgeting

Investing — Savings to be used for future expenses

Retirement Planning
Insurance Planning
Estate Planning

House   Car   Education   Children   Retirement

BUDGETING

In order to invest money, you need to have it. Most people have sources of income. Some of this gets spent paying for normal living expenses. What is left over can be invested. You can exert more control over how much money is available for investing by setting up a budget.

MANAGING TAXES

Everybody pays taxes—on their income, food, transportation, entertainment, even on the rewards of their investments. The bottom line is that taxes act to reduce your net wealth. You can potentially improve your bottom line through effective tax planning.

> *You can potentially improve your bottom line through effective tax planning.*

An example may help. Although you probably know that you must pay taxes on interest earned from money in bank accounts, certificates of deposit, and other fixed-income instruments, did you know that the interest earned from some fixed-income securities is exempt from taxes? Do you know how to compare the bottom-line returns of tax-exempt securities against taxable securities? You can use tax planning in a number of other areas as well.

RETIREMENT PLANNING

This topic should really be considered a subset of investment planning. In retirement planning, you basically attempt to forecast how long you will live, how long you will work, and how much you will need to save while you work so that you can afford a reasonable lifestyle after you retire. With a retirement plan, you earmark a portion of your income to be invested and to remain invested until you no longer work.

Even tax planning can overlap with retirement planning. Some organizations offer pension plans or capital accumulation plans—401(k) or 403(b)—where you and your employer can make pre-tax contributions. The interest, dividends, and gains from the investment of those contributions is not taxed until you retire and take money out. This affects your return in two ways: first, by deferring taxes, your money grows larger faster (through compounding); and, second, by waiting until you've retired to use the income, you will (hopefully) be in a lower tax bracket after retirement and thus end up paying less of that income to the tax man.

SETTING UP AN INVESTMENT PLAN

Of course, the part of financial planning that involves *investment* of disposable income (that is, the investment of what is left after taxes, general living expenses, insurance expenses, and retirement savings) is the part that directly applies to the scope of this book.

An investment plan takes into account a number of factors, including:

◆ time horizon

◆ return objective

◆ risk profile

◆ personal level of involvement

Time Horizon People save money to use towards a variety of goals:

◆ buying a car

◆ buying a house

◆ going on a nice vacation

◆ getting an education

◆ raising children

◆ sending children to college

Notice how these goals follow a predictable sequence for many workers. An investment plan should take into account the *time horizon* for particular investments. This term refers to the length of time between now and when you expect to spend money towards achieving a goal. If you know that you will need $5,000 six months from now for a down payment on a house, you should probably avoid investing it in risky or nonliquid securities.

Return Objective When investing money, you expect it to grow so that you have more in the future than what you started with today. If you have a goal that you are trying to reach in the future, you need to calculate the return that will be needed to achieve that goal. Different classes of investments yield different average returns. It helps to know if you can expect an investment to yield the return that you seek.

Risk Profile The return on an investment tends to be closely related to the amount of risk assumed by that investment. Over a long period of time, more risky investments tend to have higher average returns than less risky investments. This does not mean that high-risk investments always perform better than low-risk investments, or vice versa, it just means that most of the time you will have to expose yourself to more risk in order to get a higher return.

 You should be careful to examine the riskiness of an investment against its expected return. You should also ask yourself how tolerant you are of risk.

Personal Level of Involvement You also need to evaluate how active you wish to be in managing your investment plan. This will depend on three factors: your *experience* with investing, how much *time* you have available to dedicate to managing your investments, and your level of *interest*.

> *You also need to evaluate how active you wish to be in managing your investment plan.*

If you have no experience, no time, and no interest, you might consider hiring someone to actively manage your assets. (But you still need to evaluate their performance.)

If you have no experience, but do have a little time and some interest, you might consider actively managing your own investments, and focusing on mutual funds (where portfolio managers oversee the investment of the monies in their fund).

If you have all three—experience, time, and the interest—you might consider actively managing your investments across a wide range of securities.

PORTFOLIO MANAGEMENT

As you invest money, it will probably end up going into different kinds of securities. These securities might pay interest, dividends, or other types of proceeds. They might rise or drop in value. You might sell them for a loss or a gain. They might have different risk characteristics. How do you keep track of all these factors and make decisions based on the information? In part, through portfolio management.

One basic thing you do with a portfolio is keep track of where your money goes (see Figure 1.2). For example, you might have a bank account with money in CDs and a checking account; a 401(k) plan at work, where a portion of your pre-tax income gets invested in stock-and-bond mutual

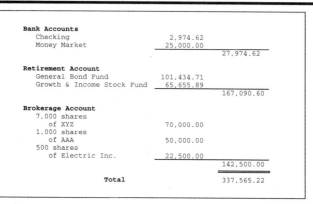

Figure 1.2:
Keeping track of your
investments

Bank Accounts		
Checking	2,974.62	
Money Market	25,000.00	
		27,974.62
Retirement Account		
General Bond Fund	101,434.71	
Growth & Income Stock Fund	65,655.89	
		167,090.60
Brokerage Account		
7,000 shares		
of XYZ	70,000.00	
1,000 shares		
of AAA	50,000.00	
500 shares		
of Electric Inc.	22,500.00	
		142,500.00
Total		337,565.22

funds; and an account at a brokerage firm where you try your hand at mastering Wall Street.

At the end of the year (or even more frequently), you might wish to know how much money you have saved in total and in which securities it is invested. You set up one or more portfolios to keep track of this information, recording all of your investment transactions.

Besides knowing how much money you have managed to save, it is a good idea to know how well the investments perform. You certainly need to have savings keep pace with inflation, but you should also know how well your investments are performing relative to other similar securities.

In addition to tracking the performance of your investments through portfolio management, you can manage your overall exposure to risk by monitoring and controlling the allocation of assets. This can be accomplished at several levels. First, you can divide investments into classes such as stocks, bonds, and cash (see Figure 1.3). Second, you can divide these classes into their own groups—stocks based on industry, bonds based on maturity, for example. This allocation of assets is often referred to as *diversification*.

Diversification is a step you can take to reduce exposure to a number of types of risk. For example, if you invest all of your money in one stock, it is exposed to a number of different risks. If the economy goes into a recession, the stock may drop in value. If the stock's industry falls under strict regulation, its value may drop. If the stock's sales fall, it may go out of business. By putting half of your money into another stock, you reduce your portfolio's exposure to the risk of that stock going out of business. If the second stock is in a different industry, you have reduced your portfolio's risk exposure to

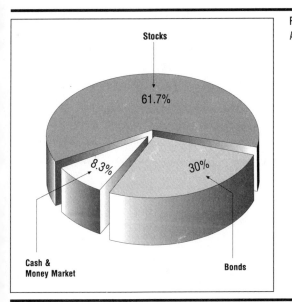

Figure 1.3:
A pie chart showing portfolio composition

Stocks

61.7%

8.3%

30%

Cash &
Money Market

Bonds

negative events in one industry. If you put half of your money in treasury bills, you have reduced your portfolio's risk exposure to negative events in the stock market overall.

Remember that you cannot completely eliminate risk. Nor should you necessarily want to: in general, lower risk exposure means a lower average return.

There is much more to portfolio management than what has been mentioned here, but you should now have a better idea about what people mean when they refer to the term. You can find more information in journals and books devoted to the subject.

FUNDAMENTAL STOCK ANALYSIS

Many people have a basic familiarity with the stock market. Companies offer shares of equity in their ownership to the public. These shares trade on exchanges. Individuals can invest in a company by purchasing shares. Typically, you cannot go to the exchange and personally buy or sell shares of a company; instead, you use a brokerage firm to transact the trade for you.

How do you determine what is a good stock and what is a bad stock? One technique involves examining the company's financial statements to determine its value. This technique is called *fundamental analysis* because it takes the company's *fundamentals* into account.

A company's financial statements are a lot like your personal bank statements, income tax forms, and other financial papers. They reveal a company's income (sales), its expenses, its savings (retained earnings), and its

Consolidated Balance Sheet			
December 31 ($ in millions except per share amounts)	1994	1993	1992
Assets			
Current Assets			
Cash and cash equivalents..	$ 875.1	$ 787.5	$ 665.4
Short-term investments..	844.0	698.1	602.8
Accounts receivable...	1,665.3	1,547.9	1,468.4
Inventories..	1,251.6	1,123.7	1,099.2
Prepaid expenses and taxes...	645.7	599.9	524.5
Total current assets...	5,281.7	4,757.1	4,360.3
Property, Plant and Equipment, at cost			
Land..	310.4	250.6	198.7
Buildings..	2,523.0	1,946.2	1,228.9
Machinery, equipment and ofice furnishings...................	4,001.6	3,936.3	3,776.5
Construction in progress...	757.9	651.4	558.2
	7,592.9	6,784.5	5,762.3
Less allowance for depreciation.......................................	2,232.1	1,984.0	1,855.7
	5,360.8	4,800.5	3,906.6
	10,642.5	9,557.6	8,266.9
Liabilities and Stockholders' Equity			
Current Liabilities			
Accounts payable and accrued liabilities.........................	$1,574.9	$ 1,512.8	$1,479.9
Loans payable...	967.6	453.4	388.1
Income taxes payable..	1,014.8	996.5	853.8
Dividends payable...	301.1	288.5	246.8
Total current liabilities..	3,858.4	3,251.2	2,968.6
Long-term debt...	513.0	486.4	453.6
Deferred taxes and noncurrent liabilities.........................	1,404.8	1,215.7	1,002.2
Total Liabilities...	5,776.2	4,953.3	4,424.4
Stockholders' Equity			
Common stock...	248.7	222.5	199.9
Retained earnings...	4,617.6	4,381.8	3,642.6
Total stockholders' equity..	4,866.3	4,604.3	3,842.5
	10,642.5	9,557.6	8,266.9

Figure 1.4: Examples: income statement and balance sheet

Consolidated Statement of Income			
Years Ended December 31 *($ in millions except per share amounts)*	**1994**	1993	1992
Sales...	**$9,678.5**	$8,502.6	$7,687.4
Costs & Expenses			
Materials and production.................................	**2,095.2**	1,933.3	1,888.2
Marketing and administrative..........................	**2,463.7**	2,615.1	2,277.0
Research and development...............................	**1,000.7**	989.0	876.1
	5,559.6	5,537.4	5,041.3
Income Before Taxes..	**4,118.9**	2,965.2	2,646.1
Taxes on Income...	**1,276.9**	978.5	899.7
Net Income..	**2,842.0**	1,986.7	1,746.4

Figure 1.4:
Examples: income statement and balance sheet (continued)

assets and liabilities. Most of this information is summarized on the income statement and the balance sheet (see Figure 1.4). This information is reported on a quarterly basis (unaudited) and annual basis (audited). Fundamental analysis is the process of examining a company based on the information contained in its financial statements. It's a process that can be divided into two steps: screening and valuation.

STOCK SCREENING

When you decide to analyze stocks based on the state of their financial condition, how do you find the stocks that deserve detailed attention? With close to 10,000 stocks listed on the New York Stock Exchange, American Stock Exchange, and NASDAQ Over-the-Counter Stock Exchange; one can't examine them all. That is where stock *screening* comes in handy.

You can use stock screening to filter out a group of stocks that share some common traits. This allows you to focus your attention on a manageable number of stocks. To set up a stock screen, you specify the common traits that you are looking for in a stock. For example, suppose you want to invest some money in conservative income stocks. You probably would want to find stocks that have an above-average dividend yield, sufficient earnings to allow this level of payment to continue in the future, and perhaps a history of positive dividend growth.

The most efficient way to accomplish fundamental stock screening is with a computer using a program to do the screening and a database to supply the fundamental data.

Once you finish the process of stock screening, you can continue with the next process, stock valuation.

STOCK VALUATION

Once you have some prospective stocks, you can proceed to study each one's fundamentals individually. This is referred to as fundamental stock valuation. The goal of this analysis is to determine the company's "fair value" and its future prospects.

Generally, people use fundamental valuation techniques to forecast the future price of the stock. A number of stock pricing models exist and their suitability varies from company to company. For example, a dividend-based pricing model can be used. However, it tends to work poorly for startup companies and high-tech companies because they do not typically pay dividends—they need to reinvest their earnings to support growth. An earnings-based pricing model works well for companies that are profitable but do not pay a dividend. If a company has had losses, an earnings-based model may not be appropriate. Also, earnings can be distorted by special charges for irregular events, such as restructurings or damages from lawsuits. A sales-based earnings model can eliminate such factors.

> *People use fundamental valuation techniques to forecast the future price of the stock.*

The above perspective applies primarily to investors interested in a company from its equity side. Institutions that lend money to companies in the form of debt also analyze their financial statements, but from a different perspective—usually their ability to make the debt payments in a timely fashion. Companies also analyze their own financial statements, from yet another perspective. Realize that the analysis of financial statements is as much art as it is science, and that the interpretation of these statements can be approached from several directions.

Remember that a company does not exist in a vacuum. This means that while a lot can be gained from studying its financial statements, you should also consider its numbers relative to those of its peers. This means studying the fundamentals of the industry in which the company competes, and the fundamentals of the market overall. This can be extended to include the economy, both national and international. (However, I break economic analysis out as its own topic because it impacts all classes of securities.) Economic analysis is explained at the end of this overview on investing.

FIXED-INCOME ANALYSIS

The previous section covered the analysis of equity securities. This section will cover a group of securities that differ greatly in nature from equity securities: fixed-income securities, which are also referred to as *debt securities*.

Let's compare the different types of securities. An *equity* security, such as common or preferred stock, represents partial ownership of an organization. When you buy shares of a stock, you are lending money in return for a share of the profits that result from the use of that money. When you buy a *fixed-income* security, you are lending money to an organization in return for a fixed payment back from the borrower, regardless of the profits that result from the use of that money. With *debt* securities, the borrower normally pays back the money you lent (principal) plus an additional amount (interest).

The return for a fixed-income security is not necessarily fixed. The return can actually change under special circumstances—for example, if you sell it before maturity, if it is repaid before maturity (referred to as callable*), or if the borrower cannot make the required payments on the specified date(s). Also, several measures of yield (a way of measuring return) assume that coupon payments can be reinvested at a fixed rate, even though rates will likely change between the date of issue and maturity.*

Federal, state, and local governments, the governments of other countries, and private companies all borrow money in the form of debt to finance their operations. Typically, debt is paid back over a time period that can range from several weeks to thirty years. Some forms of debt have lifespans (maturity) greater than thirty years, but they are rare. Debt issued with a maturity date of one year or less is called a *bill*. Treasury bills, for example, are issued with maturity dates ranging from three to fifty-two weeks. Debt issued with a maturity date between one and ten years is called a *note*. And debt issued with a maturity date over ten years is called a *bond*.

The analysis of debt tends to focus on its structure, return, sensitivity to changes in interest rates, the safety of its issuer, and any special provisions such as an early call date.

MUTUAL FUND ANALYSIS

Mutual funds are a very popular investment vehicle. A mutual fund is basically a pool of money, provided by individuals, that is managed in a variety of securities by a professional or group of professionals. Although mutual funds have existed in America throughout most of this century, their popularity has grown significantly over the past twenty years. This can be attributed to several factors, including product diversification (there are now index funds, sector funds, and country funds, for example) and an appreciating market in stocks and bonds (at least for the past ten years).

Mutual funds offer some attractive features to the individual investor. First, a fund is managed by a professional investment manager. This is a good thing, because most of us lack sufficient time or experience to properly manage a portfolio of stocks and bonds.

A mutual fund allows individuals to diversify their portfolios—even with small sums of money.

Second, a mutual fund allows individuals to diversify their portfolios—even with small sums of money (a thousand dollars minimum for most, even less for some). Mutual funds are required by law to meet various diversification requirements, both in terms of the number of different securities held and in terms of the proportion of monies invested in each of those securities.

Third, a mutual fund operates on such a large scale that its marginal costs are lower than those that an individual would incur (the same idea as the concept of small-volume/retail prices versus large-volume/wholesale prices).

And fourth, a mutual fund handles all of the administrative paperwork and sends you the summary statements. This is quite useful for those mutual funds that have high turnover ratios (a yardstick that measures how actively a fund adjusts its portfolio).

Today, thousands of mutual funds offer their services to individuals. Selecting a mutual fund therefore presents problems similar to those one confronts in selecting a stock. The general practice of *screening*, mentioned previously in the section on fundamental stock analysis, can also be used to help locate prospective mutual funds.

A useful way to screen, and analyze, a mutual fund is to look at it like a miniature portfolio. Key considerations include past performance, investment objective, portfolio composition, and charges. And like stocks, mutual funds do not exist in a vacuum, so you will find it useful to look at a fund not only in absolute terms, but in relative terms as well.

FUTURES AND OPTIONS

The use of these two classes of securities has grown significantly over the past twenty years. Futures and options are *derivative* securities. This means that their value is derived from the value of some other asset. They are generally considered high risk types of investment vehicles. While they can be used to limit risk exposure, they can also greatly increase your exposure to risk.

A *future* is a contract between two parties. In the contract, the two parties agree to trade an asset (gold, Deutschemarks, stock index) at a specific date in the future for a certain price ($400 per ounce of gold, $0.73 per Deutschemark, cash value of the index on that date). Futures are normally traded on an exchange. The exchange requires that the futures have a standard set of features, and in turn they guarantee that the contract is honored. This allows parties to trade contracts with other parties that they do not know (normally a contract is between two specific parties and is not transferable to third parties). A *forward* is a futures contract that is not traded on an exchange (there are some other fine distinctions as well).

An *option* is similar to a future. The main difference is that an option contract does not require that the two parties trade an asset in the future; it simply gives the buyer the right to do something in the future. There are two basic classes of options: *calls* and *puts*.

◆ A *call* is an option that gives its holder the right to *buy* the asset specified in the contract at a certain price by a certain date.

◆ A *put* is an option that gives its holder the right to *sell* the asset specified in the contract at a certain price by a certain date.

In either case, the holder can choose to not exercise their right. The seller of an option, however, has no choice, simply an obligation to fulfill their side of the transaction if the holder decides to exercise their right.

One other item worth noting about how options can differ from futures is in the timing of the transaction. Some options allow the holder to exercise their right at any time until the date that it expires. This type of option is called an American option. Other options only allow the holder to exercise their right on the expiration date, not before. This is called a European option. These names have nothing to do with where the options are traded. Rather, these two names refer to the time *when* the option can be exercised (should the holder choose to do so).

TECHNICAL ANALYSIS

While a security can be examined in terms of its internal characteristics, you can also analyze it in terms of its external characteristics. Technical analysis is the study of a security's price and volume behavior (and open interest behavior, where applicable). The idea behind technical analysis is basically that the market price of a security reflects its internal factors. In fact, some will claim that a technical analyst does not even need to know whether the security is a stock, bond, mutual fund, future, or option.

 You may hear people argue about fundamental and technical analysis. Each camp points out weaknesses with the other camp's methods and claims that its methods are better. It might be better to simply recognize that every method has its own set of inherent weaknesses, and focus on employing the strengths of both methods. Many people use technical analysis not so much to select securities as to determine the timing of sales and purchases of securities that have already been selected.

A PICTURE SAYS A THOUSAND WORDS

Technical analysis employs the use of charts and other graphic tools. You can learn a lot about the historic behavior of a security's price simply by graphing the information. Several choices of chart formats exist, including bar, candlestick, equivolume, line, and point-and-figure. Each format focuses on a particular aspect of a security's historic price behavior. Figure 1.5 shows a bar chart of the Dow Jones Industrial Average for the year period from January 1993 to April 1995.

You use these charts to determine such things as the overall trend of the price movement, possible levels where the trend may change direction, and other types of patterns.

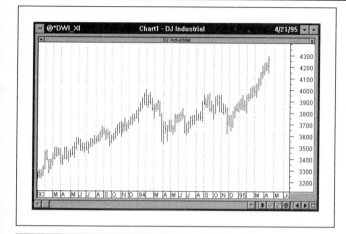

Figure 1.5:
A bar chart of the Dow
Jones Industrial Average

WORKING WITH CHARTS

You can do a number of things with a chart to help determine trend direction, reversal points, and other patterns. Trendlines and indicators provide various perspectives about a security's price movement. A trendline is drawn by connecting two or more low (or high) points on a chart to indicate the general direction of movement over a certain time span. Figure 1.6 shows the previous bar chart with two trendlines added.

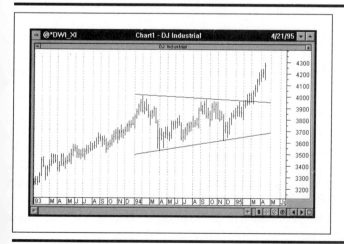

Figure 1.6:
Trendlines added to a
bar chart

Indicators are typically numbers whose value is a function of a security's price, volume, and/or open interest. Dozens of general indicators exist and each type's value can be a function of multiple parameters. The ubiquitous *moving average* indicator serves as an intuitive example. A moving average is an indicator whose value is calculated as an average of the previous number N prices. Parameters used to specify the value include simple (equally weighted) or weighted average, the number of periods to be included, and which price is used (open, high, low, or close). This may seem awfully detailed; however, the point of this description is to emphasize that technical analysis can quickly turn into a complex subject. Ultimately, the goal is to use indicators and trendlines to help improve the timing of investment decisions. Figure 1.7 illustrates a bar chart with a 30-day moving average superimposed on it.

Figure 1.7:
A 30-day moving average of the Dow Jones Industrial Average

HINDSIGHT IS 20/20

You can test the efficacy of using one or more indicators to time investment decisions by checking a security's historic performance. This is called back-testing or strategy testing. Its value is in letting you find out how well you would have done without actually risking any money; you get an idea of the risks and rewards. However, it ignores the pyschological aspects involved in making investment decisions, and its predictive value becomes more suspect as the indicators can be over-fitted to create "optimal" results.

TECHNICAL SCREENING

If you want to analyze a large number of securities using the same indicators and parameters, the previously mentioned screening technique can be used.

Computers offer a practical and efficient means of accomplishing this task.

Once again, computers offer a practical and efficient means of accomplishing this task. This form of analysis is not currently available through the Internet, but should begin to appear in the second half of 1995.

Take care, however, when applying indicators with a fixed set of parameters to multiple securities.

ECONOMIC ANALYSIS

All securities are affected by economic factors; therefore, it makes sense to consider the potential impact that these factors can exert on the performance of a security. One problem in this lofty goal is the sheer size and complexity of an economy (or of several interrelated economies for that matter).

On a large scale, an economy encompasses the overall output of goods and services, the growth of this output, inflation, unemployment, and standard of living. If you're considering several economies linked to each other, you must also include the balance of trade between those economies. Analyzing the economy at this level requires examining monetary and fiscal policies, government budgets, money supply, interest rates, labor supply, industrial capacity, and many more factors. Economic analysis on this scale is often called *macro*economics. On the flip side of the coin, *micro*economics concerns the study of a component of an economy—a particular industry, for example.

Important Financial and Investment Terms

401(k) The section of the Internal Revenue Code that defines one type of retirement plan that for-profit organizations may offer to their employees. Under this plan, an employee is allowed to contribute pretax dollars to a company investment pool.

403(b) The section of the Internal Revenue Code that defines one type of retirement plan that not-for-profit organizations may offer to their employees. Under this plan, an employee is allowed to contribute pretax dollars to a company investment pool.

AMEX American Stock Exchange

Call Option A contract that gives the holder the right to buy a specified asset at a fixed price by a certain date.

CD Certificate of Deposit. A type of fixed-income security typically issued by a bank.

CFTC Commodity Futures Trading Commission. This government organization regulates the activities of commodities exchanges in the United States.

Diversification The act of investing one's wealth in multiple classes of assets (stocks, bonds, and cash, for example). This is typically intended to reduce exposure to specific types of risk.

Future A contract to exchange an asset for a fixed price at a specified date in the future.

NASDAQ National Association of Securities Dealers Automated Quotations system, owned and operated by the National Association of Securities Dealers. It is a computerized system that allows brokers and dealers to trade over-the-counter stocks electronically.

NYSE New York Stock Exchange

Penny Stock   A stock that sells for under $1 (although some people will also include in this definition stocks with a price less than $5). This type of stock is usually issued on companies that have a short and/or erratic history of revenues and earnings. It is also usually listed on an exchange that has lax regulatory requirements.

Portfolio   A collection of investments that may include a variety of securities such as stocks, bonds, cash, mutual funds, futures, and options.

Put Option   A contract that gives the holder the right to sell a specified asset at a fixed price by a certain date.

SEC   Securities and Exchange Commission. This government organization regulates the activities of stock exchanges in the United States.

Using the Internet

Today, *Internet* is a household word. A couple of years ago, it was a fairly obscure term. This new popularity is both good and bad. It is good because the Internet offers great potential, both in the present and the future. However, this popularity is also bad, because it raises people's expectations to sometimes false highs.

One purpose of this book is to cut through the hype and glory to show the current reality of the Internet as it relates to investing. While this may not be as exciting as going for a ride at an amusement park, hopefully it will leave more money in your pocket (and help you to make that money grow).

WHAT IS THE INTERNET?

The Internet is many things. At its most basic level, the Internet is simply a bunch of computer networks connected to each other by phone lines (see Figure 1.8). Although this makes the Internet a rather technical and complex thing, one of the great things about it is that you don't need to understand its technical aspects to use it successfully. The automobile is a good analogy: you don't need to know how to tune an engine or even understand the principles behind an engine to drive your car.

SOME HISTORICAL BACKGROUND

The Internet was born in the late fifties and early sixties as a government-sponsored project under the Department of Defense. At that point it was called ARPANET (Advanced Research Projects Agency Network). The goal was to create a communications network that the U.S. defense system could depend on, regardless of malfunction or, especially, attack. A primary goal was to set up the network so that if one part was knocked out, the information flow could simply be rerouted and communications could continue.

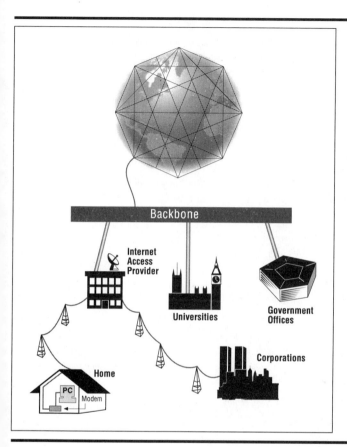

Figure 1.8:
A simple view of the
Internet

As computer technology became more commonly accessible in the late seventies and early eighties, smaller-scale networks began to grow in universities and corporations (as well as in government). In the early eighties the LAN (Local Area Network) was a phenomenon like multimedia and the Internet are today. In the mid-eighties a number of computer-literate leaders began to realize that these numerous networks could be connected to each other to elevate communication to a new order of magnitude.

At about this time, the National Science Foundation (NSF) set up a network called NSFNET. The network used many of the standards developed under the ARPANET, and the NSF encouraged educational organizations such as colleges and universities to use this network as a means of communicating with each other and with the governmental bodies that supported their research. In fact, the NSF required that universities make access to the network available to everyone within their organization—professors, students, and administrative staff. Furthermore, the NSFNET was connected to the networks in countries around the world to facilitate communication on a global scale. All of a sudden a huge number of people had the freedom to use the network as long as it pertained to "research" as defined by a policy called the Acceptable Use Policy (AUP). The NSFNET became the backbone of the Internet.

Soon, companies and private individuals wanted access to the Internet. They were hearing about the ability to send letters electronically to other people around the world, the ability to gain access to vast resources at libraries, and more. Commercial connections to the Internet sprang to existence to meet this demand. Today, dozens of commercial organizations offer access to the Internet.

INTERNET ACCESS PROVIDERS

Internet service providers, also called Internet access providers, offer Internet connections for any computer user—from large multinational corporations down to the private individual. Today, you can get full access to the Internet for approximately the same price that you would pay for a *commercial online service*, one of the publicly accessible networks that were set up independently of the Internet. For example, at the time of this writing Netcom offers a direct link to the Internet for the fixed rate of $19.95 per month, and they have phone access numbers in most U.S. cities.

> *You can get full access to the Internet for approximately the same price that you would pay for a commercial online service.*

So, you might ask, what is the difference between a commercial online service and the Internet?

◆ Online services are different from the Internet primarily in that they are typically owned by one company. Some well-known online services include America Online, CompuServe, and Prodigy. Currently, the Internet is not completely controlled by any one person, company, or government. It is quite literally a bunch of independent computer networks hooked up to each other.

◆ Most of the places you can access on the Internet are public, but some are private. The general online services are private, and on several services a number of their features require that you pay additional charges over and above the regular subscription and connect-time fees. For example, the misc.invest newsgroup is open to all Internet users; however, the Investor's Forum on CompuServe is an Extended Services feature where you are billed extra fees while using that area.

Points to consider when selecting an Internet access provider are covered beginning on page 32 under the section Finding an Internet Access Provider.

The distinction between the Internet and online services is getting blurry now because online services are offering limited Internet access to their subscribers, and will eventually offer full Internet access. (The various levels of Internet access are explained in the section Getting Connected, beginning on page 26.)

One important current distinction, however, is that *you cannot access commercial online services from the Internet* (other than to send their subscribers e-mail). In the near future, this aspect will disappear as well. Online services will offer access to their areas from the Internet, for a fee. Just how this will be priced remains to be seen. When this happens, they will have effectively become a subset of the Internet, just like any other data vendor that can be accessed via the Internet for a fee. In fact, as you will see, a good number of the investment areas on the Internet sell information as their primary service (and some areas provide the information for free).

BULLETIN BOARDS AND THE INTERNET

Electronic bulletin boards (BBSs) also deserve to be included in this discussion. A BBS is typically a remote computer site that you can access with a computer, modem, and phone line. However, it differs from the Internet and online services in several respects.

First, a BBS offers only a limited quantity of phone numbers (usually just one), and they are usually not toll-free. (If you do not live within the local calling area of the BBS, the call will be long-distance.

Second, a BBS normally has a much smaller base of users than the Internet or an online service. Some bulletin boards, however, are beginning to establish Internet connections and may develop in the same manner that online services appear to be developing with respect to accessing the Internet. So far, several government BBSs offer access via the Internet.

With this background in mind, let us examine what alternatives exist for getting connected to the Internet.

GETTING CONNECTED

This section discusses how to get set up to travel across the Internet. It also provides some more detailed information about how the Internet is physically connected, what equipment you will need (hardware and software), how to select an access provider, and what type of account to get.

You can access the Internet in a number of different ways. The type of connection you get will affect the speed with which you can perform various activities while online and will determine, to some extent, the tools that you can use to navigate and operate within the Internet.

CONNECTING THROUGH ORGANIZATIONS

You may have the ability to use a computer at work or school or someplace other than home to access the Internet. Organizations that need to provide Internet access to numerous people often have dedicated phone lines (lines dedicated solely to accessing the Internet and/or online services) and special hardware and software for managing the activities of multiple users.

In the event that you can get Internet access from such a place, you should check into the organization's policies outlining acceptable use of its computer resources before getting an account and adventuring across the Internet.

CONNECTING FROM HOME

To access the Internet from home, you will obviously need a computer. But you will also need a phone line, a modem, some communications software, and an account with an Internet access provider. The following sections provide information helpful in getting the right stuff in all of those categories.

The Computer The general rule of thumb here is "the bigger, the better." You will need a fast, powerful machine in order to navigate efficiently across the Internet. There are many levels of detail that can be considered in selecting a computer; however, the basic hardware components to focus on include:

> *The general rule of thumb here is "the bigger, the better."*

1. The CPU and its Clock Speed. I recommend a PC with a 486 CPU and a clock speed of 66 MHz (megahertz).

2. RAM Memory Capacity. I recommend at least 8 MB (megabytes).

3. Hard Disk Drive Capacity. I recommend at least a 340-MB hard drive.

The other consideration you need to make with respect to a computer is compatibility. Many Internet access programs require a minimum hardware configuration (such as having a 386 CPU or better). Before going out and buying any hardware or software and signing up for some Internet account, you should shop around for all of the items that you plan to get. Check with someone who can guarantee that they will all work properly with each other. Then go out and get them—you won't save much by scouting for the absolute lowest price if in the process you take weeks to do it. By biting the bullet, you will save yourself many headaches, a great deal of time, and probably some money.

If you do not currently own a computer and plan on purchasing one primarily for use in investment decision making, you should strongly consider purchasing an IBM-compatible PC. I have no problems with the Macintosh line of computers made by Apple; they are great. However, when you look at the market for investment software, you will soon discover that about only 20 percent of the programs will run on Macintosh computers. Let's face it, investment software developers as a whole choose to write their programs for the IBM-compatible market because it is viewed as a business computer.

Phone Lines: They're Not Just for Talking Anymore As mentioned earlier, the group of networks that make up the Internet are hooked up to each other by phone lines. These lines can vary in terms of their *bandwidth*. The larger the bandwidth, the faster you can transfer a given amount of data (think of a garden hose—as you increase the diameter of the hose, the greater the amount of water that can flow out). Table 1.1 provides a summary of telephone lines and their bandwidths.

At the highest level, special dedicated lines (called T3 lines) pass data at a rate of over 40 megabits per second. This translates to over 5 megabytes per second (one byte consists of eight bits). These lines are very expensive to manage, and few organizations use them.

In the middle of the spectrum, there are dedicated lines (T1 lines) that provide transfer rates of 1.5 megabits per second, or about 187 kilobytes per second. T1 lines are generally too expensive for individuals; however, they are cost-effective for many organizations.

At the bottom end of the spectrum is the regular voice phone that provides an average bandwidth of 14 kilobits per second, or about 1.8 kilobytes per second. This is currently the only affordable means the average individual has for accessing the Internet. These phone lines are frequently referred to as *POTS* for Plain Ordinary Telephone Service.

Although these different classes of phone lines have a maximum bandwidth, there are ways of squeezing more information through them, primarily by compressing the data. This concept is similar to that of compressing the information on your computer's hard disk drive to fit more files on it.

A special type of phone line, a digital one, that uses *ISDN* (Integrated Services Digital Network) technology offers significantly greater bandwidth than POTS lines. ISDN phone lines have bandwidths ranging from 64 to 128 kilobits per second. Regional Bell operating companies (RBOCs) have been offering this technology to commercial enterprises for a long time and are now working at offering a cost-effective service to individuals. Watch this area of technology closely over the next few years, you may see its use by households increase significantly.

Table 1.1: A Summary of Telephone Lines and Their Bandwidths		
Telephone Line	**Bandwidth**	**Equivalent in Bytes**
T1	1.5 Megabits/sec	187 Kilobytes/sec
T3	40+ Megabits/sec	5+ Megabytes/sec
POTS	14 Kilobits/sec	1.8 Kilobytes/sec
ISDN	124 Kilobits/sec	15+ Kilobytes/sec

You can expect to see this technology helping to further the use of more sound-, graphic-, and video-based features in computing. Multimedia communication on computers has not grown much yet because users are constrained by the limits of the phone lines over which they communicate. For example, one minute of high-fidelity, stereo, digitally sampled music takes about 10 megabytes of space. To listen to this in real-time, you would need an effective throughput of about 166 kilobytes per second. You couldn't use a POTS line for that kind of transmission—you would need a T1 line for it. Now suppose you wanted video as well as audio!

Selecting a Modem This is a simple step that requires almost no technical expertise and only a small investment of time and money. You can purchase a good modem for less than $150, or a high-quality modem for under $250, from a retail or mail-order store. And, as with computers, you can expect the prices to continue to drop over time. There are only a few basic facts you need to know about modems—mainly, what to look for before buying one.

First, look at the speed with which it can transfer data. Today's low-end modem transfers data at 9600 bps (you may hear people use the term "baud" which is essentially equivalent to bits per second). An intermediate-level modem will transfer data at 14,400 bps, and a high-end one transfers data at 28,800 bps. We will probably soon see modems with higher speeds; however, for now this is the basic set of choices. If you do not already have a modem, I recommend that you ignore 9600 bps ones and preferably go for the 28.8K bps modems. The reason for the high-end recommendation: you will have the ability to work with the Internet's resources more quickly.

> *Go for the 28.8K bps modems.... you will have the ability to work with the Internet's resources more quickly.*

If you have ever shopped for a modem or read an article in a magazine about them, you have probably encountered a litany of cryptic techno-lingo that brought an abrupt end to any interest that you might have had in them. Terms frequently associated with modems include MNP-5, V.34, V.Fast, asynchronous, etc. Unless you have some special needs or have an inquisitive streak in you, don't worry about what these terms mean—virtually all modems follow a standard set of specifications for a given speed of data transmission.

Another consideration you face when purchasing a modem is basically cosmetic. Do you buy an internal or external modem? They will perform equally well; however, internal and external modems have their tradeoffs. On the one hand, external modems are easier to install—you simply plug them into a slot in the back of your computer. To install an internal modem, you have to remove the computer's cover and plug a card into a slot in the motherboard. On the other hand, an external modem has to be plugged into an electrical outlet, whereas an internal modem gets its power directly from the computer. Other factors include portability, visibility, and space: an external modem is portable and an internal one isn't; you can see the status lights on an external modem but not on an internal one; an external modem takes up space outside of the computer and can be damaged; an internal one doesn't take up space and is protected by the computer's case.

For those of you interested in learning more about this piece of hardware, I suggest that you purchase a book that covers the subject in depth. Beginners (and even intermediate users) should consider *Your First Modem*, written by Sharon Crawford and published by Sybex.

Communication Software You now need to find a good communications software package. This will allow you to use the modem in a simple and intuitive fashion. It may also include a number of utility programs that enable you to take advantage of different areas on the Internet.

Communications software can be broken into several classes. The most general class includes programs that allow you to control how your modem communicates with remote computers. Popular programs in this class include Crosstalk and Procomm. These types of programs provide only a limited interface between the user and the remote computer, which is their main drawback. For example, when you connect to an Internet account using this class of program, you must either type in commands or select choices from a single menu. You do not typically have a graphic environment and the ability to use a mouse to just point and click. Figures 1.9 and 1.10 illustrate the difference in appearance between a command-line interface and a menu shell interface.

 Although both Crosstalk and Procomm come in Windows versions, the graphic interface they gain from being Windows applications only applies to the direct use of the program. Once you are connected to a remote computer, you generally have to use whatever interface that computer uses, which may be only a command line or shell interface.

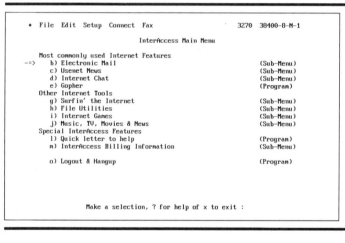

```
  •  File  Edit  Setup  Connect  Fax                3270  38400-8-N-1
OK

Welcome to InterAccess          FiberNet! NB-PM3-Port 13
   Login as guest to learn about InterAccess
   or call (708)-498-2542 for more information

login: mfister
Password:
Last login: Wed Feb  8 23:52:04 from nb-pm4
Copyright (c) 1980,1983,1986,1988,1990,1991 The Regents of the University
of California. All rights reserved.

BSDI BSD/386 1.1 Kernel #2: Thu Feb  9 16:51:56 CST 1995

How to reach InterAccess:
         Type "man phones" at any prompt for a list of phone numbers.

For a quick menu of internet programs, type 'menu' at any prompt.  If
you have questions or comments, please send email to 'help'.
You have new mail.
Usage report system temorarily disabled.

Erase set to Backspace
flowbee mfister /home?/mfister %
```

Figure 1.9:
A command-line interface. You have to type in commands for everything that you want to do. (DOS is a command-line based operating system. So is Unix. Avoid Unix if at all possible.)

```
  •  File  Edit  Setup  Connect  Fax             3270  38400-8-N-1

                       InterAccess Main Menu

      Most commonly used Internet Features
 -=>    b) Electronic Mail                          (Sub-Menu)
        c) Usenet News                              (Sub-Menu)
        d) Internet Chat                            (Sub-Menu)
        e) Gopher                                   (Program)
      Other Internet Tools
        g) Surfin' the Internet                     (Sub-Menu)
        h) File Utilities                           (Sub-Menu)
        i) Internet Games                           (Sub-Menu)
        j) Music, TV, Movies & News                 (Sub-Menu)
      Special InterAccess Features
        l) Quick letter to help                     (Program)
        m) InterAccess Billing Information          (Sub-Menu)

        o) Logout & Hangup                          (Program)



               Make a selection, ? for help of x to exit :
```

Figure 1.10:
A menu shell interface. Your choices appear as a list, much like a menu at a restaurant. (Many programs that run in DOS use a menu interface.)

While the first class of programs mentioned above are fine for the general use of modems, and are especially suitable for BBSs, a second class of communications programs offer a much better interface to the Internet—because they have been designed to work primarily *with* the Internet. For example, a number of communications packages that have recently come onto the market include a set of programs (tools) that feature an easy-to-use graphical interface to the Internet. Some programs are just bundled kits of shareware and freeware, while others have been developed as commercial packages that range in cost from $10 to over $200. For example, "Internet in a Box" is produced jointly by a group of companies that provide Internet-related products and services (you can find this package in most computer stores that sell software). This package is designed to get the beginning user hooked up to the Internet with a minimum of hassle, provide the basic set of Internet tools in a graphic interface, and all for approximately $100. I use a package provided by my local Internet access provider, InterAccess. The package they offer their customers costs $15 as of this writing, and includes a complete set of shareware and freeware Internet tools that sport a user-friendly graphical interface.

Probably the most important question to ask about this type of communications package is: What tools does it have for navigating the Internet? These are the tools that you *should* have:

◆ E-mail

◆ Newsgroup reader

◆ FTP

◆ Telnet

◆ Gopher

◆ World Wide Web (WWW) browser

The upcoming section discusses each of these Internet tools.

Some Internet access providers include the communications software along with the subscription for an Internet account, or offer a package for an additional cost in the event you don't want to have to shop for the software yourself. Netcom, for example, has a communications software program called NetCruiser. This software, which runs under Windows, is used to connect to the Internet via Netcom. It has the basic set of Internet tools, and it can automatically upgrade itself when new releases are issued. You can get more information about Netcom's programs and services by calling them at (800) 353-6600.

Before I can discuss the third class of communications software packages, we need to introduce some of the Internet access providers and the types of accounts that they offer; the two topics are that closely related.

Finding an Internet Access Provider

Part of the process of selecting communication software is evaluating what software and types of accounts an access provider offers. An easy-to-use graphical communications software package often requires a special type of account: one that allows you to access the Internet directly from your computer.

 Some Internet access providers do not offer any type of graphical interface, but do have a menu based interface. Other providers only offer a command-line interface, typically running under a Unix operating system. If you don't know Unix, avoid this interface at all costs—or plan to set aside lots of time for learning how to work within that interface and use the programs that run from it.

A plain vanilla Internet account only allows you to connect to a remote computer at the access provider's site. You must then use the tools on that remote computer to access the Internet.

Another type of Internet account not only allows you to connect to a remote computer at the access provider's site, it also allows you to communicate in such a way that you can use programs on your own computer to access the Internet directly. The advantage here is that you can learn how to use an Internet tool designed to run under your own computer's environment more quickly than you can learn to use one that runs under a different environment. This "direct access" is accomplished, in part, through the use of a special *protocol*. A protocol is what enables your computer to communicate with the Internet access provider's remote computer. Two protocols currently exist for setting up this type of Internet account: SLIP (Serial Line Internet Protocol) and PPP (Point to Point Protocol). I cannot tell you what the specific differences are between these two protocols, but I can tell you that I have used each one with the same software and I have not noticed any significant differences in end performance.

A protocol is what enables your computer to communicate with the Internet access provider's remote computer.

Most Internet access providers offer SLIP/PPP accounts with unlimited connect time for a fixed rate, normally between $20 and $30 per month. Some access providers charge a base monthly fee for a given amount of connect time, such as 10 hours, and bill you for additional connect time over the 10 hours.

The rate for additional connect time typically is higher for prime hours and lower for off-peak hours, similar to the way long-distance telephone services work.

In selecting an access provider, go with one that charges a fixed rate for unlimited connect time unless you know you won't use the Internet much. I say this because the Internet can exert a strong attraction that sucks you in for hours, without realizing it until it's too late. It is not uncommon for a person to log in intending a session no longer than 10 to 15 minutes, only to find themselves connected for several hours.

A very important point to consider when selecting an access provider is whether you have to make a long-distance phone call just to connect to its remote computer network. Long-distance phone calls can quickly make the Internet an expensive hobby, especially if you stay connected for long periods of time. If you live in a large city, you should be able to find many access providers that have local phone numbers. Some of the providers might even be located in your city.

> *Long-distance phone calls can quickly make the Internet an expensive hobby.*

However, if you live in a rural area or can't find a locally accessible provider, you might consider finding an access provider that offers a toll-free phone number or a connection through a network such as Sprintnet or MCInet. This type of access doesn't come free, and you see it reflected in slightly higher fees; however, the additional expense is more than covered by the savings in your long-distance phone bill.

You should also ask about the speed connections offered by a prospective access provider. If a service only offers 9600 bps connections, your 28.8K bps modem will only be operating at 9600 bps. Make sure that you can connect to a phone line that has a high-speed modem at the other end so that you can get the most out of your modem.

You can get a list of Internet access providers from a personal computing magazine (*Internet World* or *Computer Shopper*, for example), from a general book about the Internet, from a friend with access to the Internet, or from a general online service (America Online, CompuServe, or Prodigy).

INTERNET TOOLS

This section summarizes the current set of tools most frequently used to access resources on the Internet. You can skip this section if you already know how use e-mail, newsgroups, FTP, Gopher, World Wide Web, and other tools.

USING E-MAIL

A primary use of the Internet is to send e-mail (electronic mail) messages. These messages are similar to those you would leave on an answering machine or in a letter. Figures 1.11 and 1.12 provide an example of how one of my editors and I communicate with each other. We don't have to play phone tag, and we don't rack up long-distance phone charges (I am in Illinois, and she is in California).

```
            To: bkieran@sybex.com
          From: mfister@interaccess.com (Mark Fister)
       Subject: Book about investing on the Internet
            Cc:
           Bcc:
   Attachments:

Hi Brenda,

There sure is a lot of information available on the internet, including
investment related information. This book should really help people to
find what they are looking for on the internet!

Sincerely,

Mark
```

Figure 1.11:
An e-mail
message from
me to an editor
at Sybex

```
Return-Path: sybex!bkieran@netcom.com
Date:  Wed, 08 Feb 95 16:55:52
From: Brenda Kieran <bkieran@sybex.com>
Sender: bkieran@sybex.com
To: mfister@interaccess.com
Subject:  Re: Book about investing on the Internet
Content-Length: 1044
X-UIDL: 792310881.000


I agree--this is going to be a very useful book for a lot of people.

Have you looked through the archive of NCSA What's New pages for
useful Web sites? I was cruising around there the other night and
thought it might be worth your while to do the same.

I'll keep an eye out for especially interesting items. Have you seen
the Internet Business Directory at http://bd.ar.com/ -- it seems like
a possibility....

BTW, e-mail is a *great* way to communicate with me. I'm often much
more on top of my e-mail than my phone messages.
```

Figure 1.12:
An e-mail reply

You will find that e-mail is a basic tool that you can use in many ways when attempting to gain access to investing-related resources. Besides writing letters to *people* you want to communicate with, you can also write more or less directly to an institution's computer. Many services are set up to recognize certain standard messages to initiate service, to cancel a subscription, or to send info. Figure 1.13 shows how I used e-mail to subscribe to weekly updates from the GNN Personal Finance Center (a site that I discuss in Part Two). To speed the processing of the hundreds of requests some institutions receive every day, some of these services don't even require a "message" in the message; all they might be looking for is certain words in the "subject" line of your message.

Figure 1.13:
Using e-mail to subscribe to GNN's Personal Finance Center weekly update

My e-mail program (Eudora) looks a bit like a Windows word-processing program. If you could see the full screen, you'd notice that it has many of the same features such as cut-and-paste, find, and print. If you know how to use Word for Windows or WordPerfect, then learning to use Eudora is a breeze. You can get the freeware version of Eudora by using FTP and going to ftp.qualcomm.com and downloading the appropriate files. (FTP is discussed beginning on page 43.)

One primary advantage of e-mail is delivery time: it's minimal. You can send an e-mail message to someone on the other side of the world and they will receive it within the same day, usually.

Through your Internet account, you can send e-mail messages to anyone else with an Internet account. You can also send messages to people who have accounts with an online service like America Online, CompuServe, or Prodigy (although you will have to change the format of the address slightly to do so—read on to find out how).

What Is an E-mail Address? When you send an e-mail message to someone, you have to specify their e-mail address. This address is typically not easy to remember. For example, mfister@interaccess.com is my personal e-mail address. This address consists of two basic parts which are separated by the @ symbol. The part that appears on the left side of the @ symbol is the person's *username*. Mine is mfister. The part that appears on the right side of the @ symbol is the address of the Internet *site* at which the person has an account. I have an account with a commercial Internet access provider called InterAccess, their Internet site name is interaccess.com.

You've probably noticed that the site name consists of several parts itself, each part being separated by a period. Examining an Internet site's address can reveal useful information about that site. Many sites end with three letters after the final period; for example, the above site ends with .com. This indicates that the site is a commercial one. The following list describes some of the more common classes of sites:

.com	Commercial, like InterAccess or Dow Jones
.edu	Educational, like a college or university
.gov	Government, like an agency or department
.mil	Military, like the Air Force or Navy
.org	Nonprofit organization

The examples listed above describe the nature of the organization that manages that site. An address may also indicate something about the site's geographic location. You will occasionally see addresses that include abbreviations for countries, provinces, states, and towns.

As mentioned earlier, you can send e-mail messages to people who have accounts with a general online service. Table 1.2 shows how you modify their e-mail address so that they receive your mail from outside of the service (note that CompuServe's has a minor change—the comma in the middle of a user's account number now becomes a period):

Table 1.2: User Name Formats in Different Services		
Online Service	Username	Internet Address
America Online	mfister	mfister@aol.com
CompuServe	12345,6789	12345.6789@compuserve.com
Prodigy	mfister	mfister@prodigy.com

Message Etiquette 101

Most messages sent over the Internet resemble a part of a typical conversation. However, on the Internet you cannot see or hear the other person that you are communicating with. This means that the message carries no tone or gestures that can add meaning to the information being communicated. Be careful how you say something, because it is very easy for another party to interpret your message in a completely different way than you meant.

An example: How could you tell if someone wanted to emphasize a point? Over the Internet, this is accomplished in the extreme by using all capital letters. This is the equivalent of shouting to someone. So if you do not intend a message to be construed as a loud exclamation, avoid using all uppercase letters. (By the way, always type your e-mail addresses in lowercase—the Internet might not recognize them if you type them in uppercase.)

Another way that people convey the feeling of a message is through the use of emoticons. These are text characters that resemble an expression, usually facial. The most ubiquitous emoticon is the smiley face :-)

If you tilt your head sideways to the left, you can see that these three characters resemble a pair of eyes, a nose, and a grin. This emoticon can be used to convey wit, humor, or sarcasm. You can find listings of popular emoticons in numerous computer books and magazines.

Your "Little Black Book" An e-mail program should provide the ability to create an address book. Figure 1.14 shows my brief address book in my Eudora e-mail program. Notice that this program lets me keep track of people by nickname. Since several of my correspondents' addresses are more than twice as long as mine, it is much easier to send them mail if I can save their e-mail addresses and give them simpler names (nicknames). When creating a message, I simply select the nickname and the e-mail program substitutes the proper e-mail address.

You can do something else with this feature: create a *mailing list*. Suppose you have a group of friends that you share ideas or meet with on a frequent basis. Wouldn't it be nice if you only had to type one letter and could send a copy of that letter to each of them? You can do this by creating a nickname for that group. Then, instead of specifying all the group

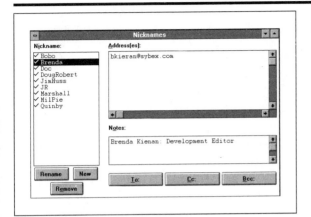

Figure 1.14:
My "Little Black Book"

members' e-mail addresses, you simply specify the group name. This is usually referred to as a mailing list.

Attaching Files to Letters Something else you can do with e-mail is *attach a file* to a message. This facility is of only limited use, however: it is mainly useful to individuals who are using the Internet via a general onlne service that does not offer FTP (*file transfer protocol,* discussed beginning on page 43). For example, at the time of this writing, America Online users can only attach files to messages addressed to other America Online members, Prodigy users can only attach files to messages addressed to other Prodigy members, etc.

If you and your correspondents have Internet accounts with full access privileges, you will probably find FTP more useful than e-mail for sending and receiving files.

USENET NEWSGROUP READERS

The Usenet is a publicly available resource on the Internet. It is the equivalent of the forum areas available with online services or the message areas on BBSs. The purpose behind these newsgroups is to serve as public areas where people can discuss topics of shared interest. People post messages that contain either questions or statements. Most often, a post will start as a question. Other people reading that message can then post a reply in the same newsgroup. Figure 1.15 shows a message that recently appeared in the newsgroup misc.invest (a newsgroup discussed in more detail in Part Two). In the message shown, one person is replying to another person's question regarding how to purchase Treasury bills. The original post is included at the beginning of the reply and is set off by a ">" arrow at the beginning of each line to indicate that it is part of a previous message. A good newsreader program will automatically insert such a character, called a "comment character," when you first select the message for reply, and most let you specify the comment character(s) you want to use. This is a still-evolving convention: some people choose something other than a ">" arrow.

From: Billman <billman@rain.org>
Subject: Re: Buying T Bills HOW?
Date: 7 Feb 1995 07:30:36 GMT

ben.leaman@labb.com (Ben Leaman) wrote:
>
> Could someone give me some info on how I can go about buying T-Bills
> myself or at the least possible cost?
> Thanks!
> Ben Leaman
> ---
> . Via ProDoor 3.4R
>
> ----
> Origination - Lancaster Area Bulletin Board - (717) 394-1357
> Internet Mail and News feeds provided by ClarkNet - Gateway to the Internet
> For info call (410) 730-9768 and login as "guest"
Buying US Gov. Securities

U.S. Treasury securities can be purchased at the auction either directly from the government or through your local brokerage.

In order to purchase U.S. Treasury securities from the government you must establish a Treasury Direct account. This can be done by mail or in person through a local Federal Reserve bank (under "Banks" in the phone book). Since the U.S. Treasury no longer issues certificates your securities will be held in electronic form (book entry) and interest payments will be wired to your account every six months. When the security matures you will be wired your principal as well.

Your broker can also make the purchase for you at the auction and save you the trouble of setting up an account as well as providing one central place for all your interest income. Most brokerages charge a fee of $50.00 and up for this service.

The Treasury auction schedule is as follows:

T-Bills
        The Treasury auctions 3-month and 6-month T-bills every Monday. One year bills are
        auctioned monthly. There is a $10,000 minimum on these purchases.
T-Notes
        Two and five year notes are auctioned the last business day of the month. The three and ten
        year notes are auctioned quarterly. The minimum on notes of five years or less is $5000 and
        $1000 for notes over five years.
T-Bonds
        The thirty year T-bond is auctioned every August and February with a $1000 minimum.

billman@rain.org

I have a personal finance homepage set up with other info at
http://www.rain.org/~billman/index.html

Figure 1.15:
A typical Usenet
newsgroup message

The quality of these postings varies greatly, from informed and professional to ignorant and immature. If the newsgroup is moderated, the moderator is responsible for ensuring that an orderly code of conduct is followed by its subscribers. Because most newsgroups go unmonitored, however, you will frequently see a high ratio of noise (pointless banter) to conversation. Of course, one person's floor is another person's ceiling. You must ultimately be the judge of what might be quality versus what might be junk.

When you view a listing of newsgroup messages, the most important details of each message normally appear on one line. This line usually includes the name of the person or group who posted the message, the number of lines in the message, and the subject (title) of the message. You can scan this information, particularly the subject/title, to locate potentially interesting messages, thereby avoiding the chaff. Of course you might still miss a good message or view a piece of junk.

Some of the Usenet newsgroups have a reputation for hosting fiery and occasionally hostile conversation. The term flaming refers to the act of one person belittling or threatening or otherwise hassling another individual. This occurs in various shades of gray. In most areas, this behavior is considered poor manners—in Internet terms, bad netiquette.

Organization The Usenet newsgroups are organized somewhat differently from the way that forums are organized within online services. Usenet is organized as a hierarchy, similar to a family tree or the layout of a computer's files in directories. At the highest level, the newsgroups are divided into large groups based on general subject matter. Although not always intuitive, these groups include such popular subjects as:

alt	alternative
biz	business, marketing, advertisements
comp	computer
misc	miscellaneous
clari	news
rec	recreational
sci	science of all types

Each group has its own subgroups, and the subgroups sometimes have their own subgroups. For example, there is a newsgroup named misc.invest.technical which is dedicated to covering discussions about technical analysis.

Newsreaders You will need a tool known as a *newsreader* to access and reply to the Usenet newsgroups. Using the newsreader, you first "subscribe" to a newsgroup to participate in it. This process of subscribing does not cost any money, like a subscription to a newspaper or magazine does; it simply activates you. With my newsreader, I just select the Subscribe menu command and the program opens a window that contains several list boxes, as illustrated in Figure 1.16. I select the appropriate category in one list box, scroll down the list of subgroups for that category in a second list box, and click on the newsgroups that I want. (If I already know the name of the newsgroup I want, I can use the Search feature to shorten the list I have to scroll through.) You can also "unsubscribe" from a newsgroup that you already subscribe to, in order to discontinue receiving its messages.

Different types of newsgroup readers are available. Usually they come bundled with the other standard Internet tools discussed here. They all provide the basic set of features, but many have "bells and whistles" (cool extra features). For example, some newsreaders enable you to keep track of topics

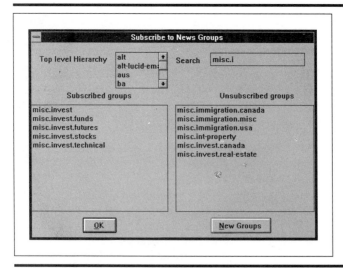

Figure 1.16:
A window for subscribing to newsgroups

over time using a feature known as *threading*. There are also minor differences from one newsreader to another. Most have adjustable word-wrap settings, but some don't. Others don't support the PgUp and PgDn keys on your keyboard, so you must rely on the mouse to scroll up or down in a message. I recommend that you check computer and Internet magazines for reviews of newsreader programs.

FAQs Because new subscribers to a newsgroup regularly post the same basic questions that other new subscribers have already posted countless times in the past, someone usually creates an FAQ (Frequently Asked Question) list that contains "answers" to these questions.

FAQ lists exist as one or more files, depending on the length of the list. An FAQ list will occasionally be posted as a message to its newsgroup, especially after an update. However, because of their length and format, it is more typical to retrieve the FAQ list as a file, by using one of the other Internet tools. FTP, which is discussed in the next section, is a common means. Other tools include Gopher and World Wide Web programs. These tools are covered later in Part One.

While the answers in an FAQ list are usually correct, there are usually no guarantees as to their accuracy (or timeliness).

FTP

As you may know, there are many locations on the Internet that offer programs, reports, articles, FAQ lists, and many other types of information, as files. You can retrieve these files using FTP.

The acronym FTP stands for File Transfer Protocol. This tool was developed at an early stage, when the Internet was still called ARPANET. Its purpose was, and still is, to facilitate the delivery of files from one computer site to another, geographically remote, computer, allowing researchers to conduct their work more efficiently.

Its purpose...is to facilitate the delivery of files from one computer site to another.

As with the other tools you see illustrated in this book, different FTP programs work differently. Figure 1.17

shows the results of an FTP session on my machine, where I downloaded the six-part FAQ list for the misc.invest newsgroup using the freeware FTP program included with the communications software kit that I ordered from my Internet access provider. A few items are worth noting in this figure. My computer's local file directory is shown in the list box on the left side of the window. The remote computer's file directory is shown in the list box on the right side of the window. I can navigate through the remote system's file directory simply by clicking on the appropriate line. Read the sidebar following this illustration to see how some names can be problematic to retrieve. To transfer a file over to my computer, I just click on the file's title and then click on the button that shows the arrow that points to my computer's file list (the left-pointing arrow, located between the two list boxes).

> *To transfer a file over to my computer, I just click on the file's title and then click on the button that shows the arrow that points to my computer's file list*

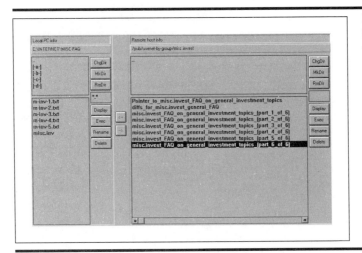

Figure 1.17:
FTP session to retrieve the misc.invest FAQ list

Warning: Retrieving Files with Long File Names

When retrieving files with long file names, many FTP programs automatically truncate the names to eight (or even fewer) characters, to conform to DOS file-naming conventions. Unfortunately, if the first eight characters of a long file name are identical from one file to the next, as happens in the list on the right in Figure 1.17, the truncated file names will also be identical. If your FTP program doesn't automatically rename each file you retrieve by including a sequence of numbers in the file names, you must download the files one at a time and then rename each file yourself before you retrieve the next one; otherwise the next, identically named, file you retrieve will overwrite the one you just retrieved.

This is something that you just learn with experience. How did I know this time around to rename the files before they got overwritten? The first clue was the length of the file names on the remote computer: because they were longer than eight characters I knew they were going to be truncated. I paid attention to the first file name after I retrieved it to see how the program was going to rename the file. When I saw that the first file was automatically renamed to misc.inv, I got suspicious and renamed it m-inv-1.txt. It turned out that each following file was also named misc.inv (in Figure 1.17 you can see the latest retrieved file at the bottom of the list on the left), so it was a good thing that I renamed each new file using a different identifying number between downloads.

Public versus Private: Anonymous FTP   Not all sites offer their information free of charge. Some locations require that you have an account set up with the individual or organization that manages that site. This is typically the case with a commercial organization whose purpose is to provide information. Once you set up an account, you will be given a username and a password. Each time you retrieve information from that service you are billed for the information that you obtained from them. Sometimes you will also be charged for the length of time that you stay connected to their site.

The Internet does have a very large number of public sites that offer their resources free of charge, however. You can access these sites using FTP and retrieve as many files as you want without paying a single cent. You do not need an account with the person or organization that manages the site to access these areas. Instead of having a username and password, you simply use the word *anonymous* for a username and enter your e-mail address as the password. The remote site then knows where to send the files that you request.

Using FTP You must know several basic things in order to successfully use FTP when retrieving (or sending) files. First, you will need to know the site's address. For example, to get copies of reports that publicly listed companies file with the SEC, you can access a site whose address is town.hall.org. This is the address for the popular EDGAR files which are discussed in the "Fundamental Stock Analysis" section of Part Two.

Second, you will need to know the names of the files you wish to download. You may not know the names in advance, but this is okay. Once you have accessed the site, you can have it list the names of the files that it contains (a site may have numerous subdirectories for storing data).

A third item that you need to be aware of is file formats. Different types of file formats exist on different computing systems. A file that works under one system probably won't work on a different system. When you use FTP, you can retrieve and send files in either binary mode or ASCII (American Standard Code for Information Interchange) mode. Using FTP in binary mode results in a file being transferred exactly as it exists in the program that created it, with special formatting and all. This is most useful for files created with commercially successful word processing, spreadsheet, and database programs, because most of them can translate each others' files. A downside to binary mode is that it makes for a larger file. If you're trying to save download time or storage space, you can use ASCII mode when transferring text files—but be aware that you won't get any formatting (like bold, italic, foreign accents, column layout, or even different sizes of type for headlines, etc.), and that any formatting codes that are a part of the file may just show up on your screen as hieroglyphics. When in doubt, you are best off using binary mode.

TELNET

Occasionally you will want to access an Internet site and do more than transfer files. For example, you might want to access a library site to run a program that searches for all articles written about a particular subject. The

Telnet tool will let you log in to that library's Internet site and use its computer and programs to perform a variety of procedures.

You can use Telnet to access public and private Internet sites. By definition, private sites require that you first open an account with them. This is normally accomplished by logging in to their site as a guest, selecting an option to register with them, and entering information about yourself (such as real name, postal mailing address, and phone number), and choosing a username and password. Then you are charged for using their services. Charges can vary greatly. You may use their computer for hours to search for a document and be billed nothing if you ultimately retrieve nothing. You might upload data to a supercomputer, have it processed, and pay a fee based on how much of their computer's time you used. These are but two examples of the many ways that you can use Telnet and be charged for such activity.

 Be sure to understand the site's pricing policy, if they have one, before doing anything at a Telnet site. This is especially true if you must provide a credit card number in advance, because you could end up with a surprise on your next monthly statement.

Telnet is a relatively crude tool because all it does is let you connect to a remote computer on the Internet. You are in effect using that remote computer's programs under that computer's operating system. These programs naturally vary in terms of their ease of use; usually you must use a command-line interface or a menu shell. Ultimately, the usefulness of Telnet depends on the quality of the programs that a remote computer has to offer.

> *The usefulness of Telnet depends on the quality of the programs that a remote computer has to offer.*

GOPHER

Gopher is really a compound tool. By that I mean it helps you use other tools more easily. For example, you can use Gopher to access remote computers and retrieve files without having to type any cryptic commands. Gopher programs give you a menu of choices, you select one (some versions let you use a mouse, others require you to enter a letter or number), and it issues all of the commands to execute the appropriate actions.

Figure 1.18 shows a listing of financial publications that I found by using Gopher. To read a sample of one of the publications, I would just select the particular choice. To get to this level, I had to navigate my way down through a series of directories. When I started my Gopher program I chose the listing Recommended Neat Gopher Servers (Try This). I then chose Electronic Newsstand from out of more than twenty listings. Within this directory I selected Business And Finance Center. From that I selected Business Publications On The Electronic Newsstand and went on to pick Finance, Real Estate, And Investing, which then displayed the choices in Figure 1.18.

This is a good illustration of why the Internet is sometimes perceived as being strange and confusing. A good analogy is what it's like when you move to a new city—you don't know where things are and it's hard to find your way around. But over time, you get familiar with the neighborhoods and you learn where to find the sources of information that answer most of your questions.

One limitation of Gophers is that they only allow you to find out about publicly available resources on the Internet—private Internet sites are not included in its listing of resources. And some Gophers are set up to give different degrees of access to different individuals. For example, a university Gopher server may not allow you to access it during peak hours because the facility is primarily intended to benefit the university's community of students, professors, and research staff.

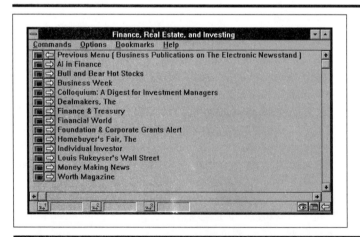

Figure 1.18:
Using Gopher to find
financial publications

Gophers and Client-Server Technology Gopher is also a compound tool in that it consists of a program which you run and a remote directory of resources on the Internet. This relationship exemplifies the concept of *client-server technology* (a popular, high-growth area of computer technology). The basic idea behind the client-server relationship is that you have a central computer, the *server*, with a variety of information and processing resources which provides access to remote computers, the *clients*, that want to use the server's resources. In the case of Gopher, you use your Gopher program, the client, to contact a Gopher resource directory, the server. The Gopher server sends back a menu listing of the resources it tracks. You make a selection, and your Gopher client relays the command back to the server.

Although technically you need to know the Internet address for the Gopher server, many Internet access providers have a Gopher client that already has the addresses of popular Gopher servers (as illustrated previously in Figure 1.18). So, most of the time, you just start Gopher and go. This tool is very fun to use because you don't have to know much in advance—you can just go out and explore the Internet resources listed by a Gopher server.

WORLD WIDE WEB BROWSERS

Like Gopher, the World Wide Web (WWW) also uses a client-server architecture, except in this case your program is called a *browser* and the server is a *Web* site. It also handles the detailed commands for doing things like logging in to remote sites and retrieving files.

The Web uses a hypertext-based system of organization rather than a menu-based one. The difference is that a menu-based structure tends to be organized as a path that splits into parallel paths that never intersect, whereas a hypertext-based structure is organized as a path that splits into numerous paths that can intersect with each other and connect to other structures as well.

Second, many Web servers present information in a rich mixture of media. Provided that you have the proper kind of browser and hardware, you will not only see text, you will also see pictures and hear sounds! Browsers with this multimedia capacity have a graphic interface that allows you to point and click your way through the Internet. Figure 1.19 shows the

Many Web servers present information in a rich mixture of media.

New York University EDGAR Project

Welcome to the EDGAR Development Project at the NYU Stern School of Business. This project is sponsored by the National Science Foundation and is undertaken in conjunction with the Internet Multicasting Service (IMS). We wish to express our appreciation to Illustra for an object-relational database grant and to RR Donnelley and Sons for their continued support. The general goal of our EDGAR development work is as follows.

To enable wide dissemination and support all levels of user access to the corporate electronic filings submitted to the Securities and Exchange Commission (SEC). Goals (continued...)

Get Corporate SEC Filings using NYU or IMS Interface

Corporate Profiles! Now with inline Performance Graphs in selected Proxies.

Frequently Asked Questions

The RR Donnelley Library of SEC Materials

Figure 1.19: EDGAR's home page on the Web

EDGAR *home page* (its starting screen) on the Web. Right away you can see that the interface is much more appealing. By improving the aesthetics, Web browsers can make the Internet less intimidating and more enjoyable.

You need to know a few things to connect to a Web. For example, the full address for the EDGAR site is:

http://edgar.stern.nyu.edu/edgar.html

The http stands for HyperText Transfer Protocol. It is like other protocols: it manages the communications between you (client) and the Web (server). The next section, edgar.stern.nyu.edu, specifies the address of the Internet site where the Web server is located. In this case, it is the EDGAR project at the Stern School of Business at New York University. The last part, edgar.html, specifies the Web server program. HTML stands for HyperText Markup Language—that's the language that specifies how data will appear and how it is cross-linked.

A Web address, like the one mentioned above, is called a URL (Uniform Resource Locator). Usually, a Web browser will already have at least one URL included in its directory. For example, my Internet access provider helps to make it easier for subscribers to find out what's available by setting up the Web browser with the URL's for a few interesting sites, including:

NCSA Mosaic's "What's New" Page

CERN Home Page

InterAccess Home Page

National Center for Atmospheric Research

Electronic Visualization Lab

Library of Congress Vatican Exhibit

Global News Network Home Page

Beginner's Guide to HTML

You can enter your own favorite Web addresses as you discover them. The process is similar to opening a spreadsheet file from Excel or Lotus and entering the information you want. Just be sure to include all of the URL's symbols, including colons and forward slashes and periods, in the proper order. And keep everything in lowercase lettering unless you see it listed otherwise.

One downside about Web servers is that some include so many detailed graphics that their pages take a while to transfer to your browser. If you have a 9600 bps modem or connect to the Internet via a 9600 account, you will likely find many Webs to be a large time sink.

Part Two: Investment Resources on the Internet

Personal Financial Planning

The Internet sites that offer financial planning resources tend to focus on the investment planning aspects of tax and retirement planning, and to some extent on estate planning. Within this section on personal financial planning I've listed the sites alphabetically, just as I will do in each of the following sections of this part of the book (there are ten sections altogether).

You will find that some of the sites I've included in this first section of Part Two provide information useful to other areas of investing, such as portfolio management or economic analysis. In such cases, the site is also covered in those later sections, as appropriate. To avoid redundancy, only the pertinent aspects are covered in a given section.

Electronic Journal of Investing

e_invest@vm.temple.edu

This site uses e-mail as its sole means of communication. It actually uses a mailing list server (the address is given in the next paragraph) to distribute e-mail messages to everybody who has signed up for the list. Any e-mail sent to the address shown above will be relayed to *all* subscribers of e_invest.

You can subscribe to this list free of charge; however, you have to pay attention to detail. It's the list server that maintains the list of subscribers, so you must send a message to the list server in order to subscribe to e_invest. Specifically, send an e-mail message to listserv@vm.temple.edu. In the body of the message, enter the text subscribe e_invest. When the list server receives your message, it will add you to the list of e_invest subscribers and it will send you a reply that contains useful instructions. Once you are on the list, you will receive every message that gets sent to the address e_invest@vm.temple.edu. If you want to post a question or reply to one, just send a message to 5.

This electronic journal contains a good interchange of information, ideas, and experiences from the people that participate. Discussions cover everything relating to investing. Topics recently covered include questions about specific securities, portfolio management techniques, sources of data, dividend reinvestment plans, and dollar cost averaging. This area shares a number of similarities with the various newsgroups pertaining to investment planning. However, it also has some tradeoffs. One primary benefit is that the journal doesn't have anywhere near as much garbage as the newsgroups tend to have. On the down side, the journal does not have as much activity as the newsgroups.

Fidelity Investments Information Center

 http://www.fid-inv.com/

Although Fidelity's Web page focuses on mutual fund analysis (discussed later, in the Mutual Fund Analysis section), it also provides some financial planning information.

The *Investor Tools* area of the Web page has several features that provide financial planning resources. *Fidelity FundMatch* is a questionnaire that asks you general investment planning questions (return objective, risk tolerance, and time horizon). The questionnaire is well designed and gets you to think about the basic aspects of investment planning; however, it only returns suggestions on mutual funds as investment vehicles.

Another feature is the *College Savings Calculator*. You are presented with information about how the calculator generates values to estimate future costs of college and the payments needed to meet those costs. You must enter the child's age, the current cost estimate for college expenses, and the investment return you aim to achieve. The calculator then generates estimates for the annual and total college expenses in the future, the required current lump sum payment, and the required annual/quarterly/monthly payments to meet this future expense.

> *The College Savings Calculator generates values to estimate future costs of college and the payments needed to meet those costs.*

You can also request that Fidelity mail you their College Savings Planning Kit for further information. This is a simple and enlightening feature.

The Investor Tools area also has an FAQ list about Investing. This hypertext list provides answers to questions about personal financial planning, portfolio management, and mutual fund analysis. A good place for beginners to examine.

GNN Personal Finance Center

http://gnn.com/gnn/meta/finance/index.html

GNN stands for the Global Network Navigator. It is a World Wide Web based resource, was created by O'Reilly & Associates, and is funded by a number of sponsors. You may currently access GNN at no cost. It consists of multiple centers, one of which is the Personal Finance Center (see Figure 2.1). This area has guests, interviews, articles, news, and pointers to investment areas on the Internet.

Some Web browsers may already have this URL included in their address book. For example, O'Reilly and several other sponsors of GNN market a package called "Internet in a Box," which contains, among other things, tools for accessing various areas on the Internet. Their Web browser has a *hotlist* that includes GNN's URL, along with others. A hotlist is a list of names for Web pages, where each name refers to a specific URL.

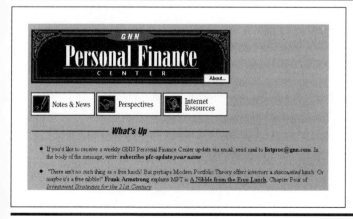

Figure 2.1:
GNN's Personal Finance Center is an outstanding place to learn more about personal finance and related sites on the Internet.

You will find that many World Wide Web sites have hypertext links with other related sites. You can automatically jump from site to site just by selecting the hypertext link. Most links are discernible because they appear in blue lettering, while the normal text appears in black lettering. Sometimes a graphic (frequently outlined in blue) acts as a link to another site.

Guests Each month, GNN's Personal Finance Center has a guest "speaker." This individual is usually a professional with experience in some field related to investing. Past guests have included several Certified Financial Planners and an economist. Individuals send their questions via e-mail to the guest. The question and following response from the guest are then posted for all other visitors to read. The Personal Finance Center also keeps historical discussions in an archive area for reference. So far, I find the guests' input to be valuable to the visitors. They give good advice, provide useful background information to their answers, cite good sources of information for further exploration on the part of the visitor, and instill a positive attitude.

Interviews In a similar vein to the guest dialogues with visitors, the Personal Finance Center publishes interviews with various individuals. The interviewees tend to be directly involved with the development of investment areas on the Internet. The list includes Chris Lott, preparer of the FAQ list for the misc.invest newsgroups (mentioned below); Mark Ginsburg, a Webmaster for the EDGAR project (covered in the section on Fundamental Stock Analysis); and Rob Frasca, cofounder of GALT Technologies and its NETworth mutual fund site (covered in the Mutual Fund Analysis section).

> *I like one feature in this area: the hypertext links....This link can be selected to go right to the Internet site that pertains to that subject.*

The interviews provide useful background information for the most part, especially the ones with individuals working on the Internet. I like one feature in this area: the hypertext links. In several interviews, a hypertext link appears right after a subject has been discussed. This link can be selected to go right to the Internet site that pertains to that subject.

Articles Periodically, the Personal Finance Center features an article about any number of investing topics. Past articles have discussed general dangers about investing, factors to consider when investing overseas, the history of the Federal Reserve, and how derivatives and hedge funds work. The articles are interesting and accurate for the most part (one article about derivatives made some generalizations that I think should have been clarified). As of the last time that I perused the articles, I liked the Federal Reserve article by Calvin Wolfe best. It explained the creation of the Fed, its purpose, how it fits into the political picture, and what it has done over the past ten years and how these actions have affected the stock, bond, and other markets.

Other The Personal Finance Center also has news updates and pointers to other investment resources available on the Internet. The news updates contain a variety of information, the most useful pertaining to new resources on the Internet. The pointers allow you to quickly and simply wander through the net to check out various investment sites. While useful, almost every investment-related web has a similar set of pointers to the same set of sites.

You can register with GNN to receive a weekly update of what's happening at the Personal Finance Center. GNN sends you the update via e-mail. To register for the update, send an e-mail message to listproc@gnn.com and in the body of the e-mail message, enter the text subscribe pfc-update your-first-name your-last-name. Figure 2.2 shows how I subscribed for the weekly update.

You can also register with GNN. This does not cost anything, but it helps GNN to continue to receive funds from its sponsors (by showing that more people are using the area). GNN has advertising for a variety of products and

```
         To: listproc@gnn.com
       From: mfister@interaccess.com (Mark Fister)
    Subject:
         Cc:
        Bcc:
Attachments:

subscribe pfc-update Mark Fister
```

Figure 2.2:
How to subscribe to GNN's weekly Personal Finance Center update

services. The nice thing is that they do not weave these ads throughout every-thing; you must choose to go to an area specifically set up for providing ads and other related information (and these areas contain useful and valuable information—they are not just a bunch of fluff). You can subscribe to GNN from their Web page, or send an e-mail message to info@gnn.com (you don't even need to say anything in the body of the message) and you will receive a reply message with instructions.

Abbot Chambers is the Editor of the Personal Finance Center and he deserves credit for developing a well-rounded facility. By the way, GNN also has centers for several other general areas—you might find their other centers useful for exploring the Internet.

IRS Web

http://www.ustreas.gov/treasury/bureaus/irs/irs.html

I think it's safe to say that few people will look forward to spending a lot of time at this Internet site (shown in Figure 2.3). This is not to say that the site lacks value or usefulness, it's just that most people don't like spending

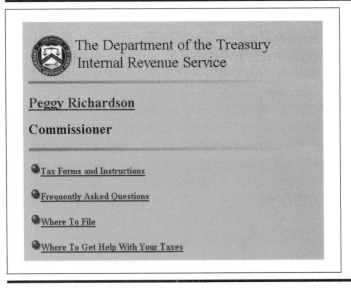

Figure 2.3:
This IRS web site isn't likely to make the top ten most popular list, but it's worth investigating anyway.

much time thinking about parting with a significant portion of their hard-earned money.

IRS Web is fairly undeveloped at this point. The largest area has copies of tax forms. You must download a free copy of Adobe's Acrobat program and set it up on your own computer in order to view the forms. However, I followed the instructions as closely as I was able, and was unable to view any of the forms properly. I am not perfect, but I have been using computers for over ten years. If I had trouble setting this up, chances are a good number of other people will too. Perhaps by the time this book is printed things will have changed.

misc.invest

misc.invest

This area is interesting to say the least. As a newsgroup, `misc.invest` generates a reasonably large volume of postings (over 100 per day). The quality of these postings covers the entire spectrum, from good to bad. While you can learn and contribute with many people via this newsgroup, you must learn how to use the area effectively. Be careful in judging the comments of others.

I would recommend that you use misc.invest not as an end source of information, but as a place to get started. In particular, you will find this area useful in learning about new investment-related resources on the Internet. It is also a good place to brainstorm and get feedback from other people and their experiences.

People post questions of all sorts in this newsgroup, sometimes barely even pertaining to the subject of investing. Participants do carry on good discussions about such topics as buying insurance, what personal finance program is best, and how 401(k) programs work. You will, however, frequently see individuals posting various kinds of schemes that range from fraudulent rip-off scams like Ponzi schemes and pyramid plans to hyping penny stocks on questionably regulated exchanges such as the Vancouver Stock Exchange.

The next entry can be considered, in some ways, the cream of the crop from this newsgroup.

The Motley Fool

The penny stock discussions got so out of hand last year that some folks who publish an electronic newsletter called *The Motley Fool* created a spoof to poke fun at the hyping scams. The spoof was designed to have the same look and feel of commonly posted hypes. In this case, the fictitious stock (Zeigletics) supposedly sold portable toilets, plungers, and bathroom deodorants and were introducing their products to countries in East Africa. The series of postings were hilarious, reading just like a story from a Monty Python movie.

Sadly, many readers bought the story—hook, line, and sinker—and a number of people, presumably the actual hypesters, responded with threats and insults. These series of events received so much notoriety that the *Wall Street Journal* even carried a story about it on the front of their "Marketplace" section (Thursday, April 21, 1994). In my opinion, the authors of the *Motley Fool* are to be commended for their creative and humorous means of drawing attention to abusive practices taking place in various online investment groups. If you want to contact the people at *The Motley Fool* to learn more about them, send an e-mail message to motleyfool@aol.com.

misc.invest FAQ List

mail-server@rtfm.mit.edu

rtfm.mit.edu

Frequently Asked Question (FAQ) lists help reduce repetitive discussions in newsgroups. The concept works particularly well with the misc.invest newsgroups because of their high volume of postings. This FAQ list contains approximately 70 to 80 pages of reference type information on investing.

The FAQ list is posted (in six separate parts) on a monthly basis in the misc.invest and misc.invest.stocks newsgroups. You can obtain a copy from several other sites too. Perhaps the simplest way to get a copy is by sending an e-mail message to the address listed at the beginning of this entry and enter the phrase

```
send usenet/news.answers/investment-faq/general/*
```

in the body of the message. The method for obtaining the list via FTP is used as an example in Part One under the FTP section.

The FAQ list has brief writeups on a number of topics including life insurance, buying versus renting, the Uniform Gifts to Minors Act (UGMA), investment information sources, 401(k) plans, IRA accounts, and investment software. I recommend getting a copy of this—it is free and, obviously, answers a number of common questions.

A gentleman by the name of Chris Lott can be thanked for starting this FAQ list. He currently functions as the list's compiler, taking additions and modifications from people and updating the list. You can send him comments and submissions via e-mail at lott@informatik.uni-kl.de.

misc.taxes

misc.taxes

This newsgroup covers, you guessed it, taxes. Activity is moderate to heavy and discussion ranges from *flame* wars (hostile exchanges between angry or upset participants) about the morality of taxation to methods of calculating the cost basis of realized gains/losses on investments. I find that this area has a high noise ratio—a lot of junk and too little quality, but this changes over time.

Modern Portfolio Management

http://www.magibox.net/~mpm

This site is discussed primarily in the Portfolio Management section of Part Two of this book. However, it provides some resources for other areas of investing, including financial planning. The services available from this Web page are all free.

The MPM Web page has a retirement savings questionnaire in its *Financial Planning Center* area. You can fill out the questionnaire while online and submit it. The service will analyze your answers and send you a report via the U.S. Postal Service (*snail mail*). The questionnaire focuses on information such as inflation expectations, your estimate of post-retirement living expenses, current age, and desired age of retirement.

NestEgg Magazine

http://nestegg.iddis.com/

The NestEgg magazine is published by Investment Dealer's Digest (IDD). Figure 2.4 shows the NestEgg Web site. The history behind IDD, the set of products they offer, and the organizations that use these products is interesting and enlightening. Information about this is available to read under the **IDD Products** section of the NestEgg web. I think reading about their background will give you some insight about how the information markets work in the investment industry.

More germane to personal finance, however, are the back issues posted under the **NestEgg Index** area. I found eight past issues available, in what appears to be their entirety (minus the ads), with the most recent issue being about three to four months old. The issues contain excellent articles. The magazine leans heavily towards covering mutual funds (not surprising,

Figure 2.4:
Look at this web page for a wealth of personal finance information—it is especially useful for beginners.

considering that most of the magazine's "advertisers" are mutual fund companies), but they certainly address the general issues pertaining to personal finance and investing. For example, one article discussed the differences between term and cash value life insurance policies. Knowing little about the world of insurance, I learned a lot from this article. The information presented is accurate, informative, and easy to understand. I strongly recommend this resource for people new to the area of financial planning and investing.

> *The information presented is accurate, informative, and easy to understand.*

NestEgg also has a *Resource Center* area on their Web. Within this area, there exists a catalog for products offered by the New York Institute of Finance. The catalog includes information about books, cassettes, videos, and other training materials. You can search the catalog by author or subject. Although the products, individually, tend to have a specific focus, the catalog provides good breadth.

The NestEgg Web also contains information relating to other areas of investing. Check the index at the back of this book to find the other sections where I cover these aspects of NestEgg.

Personal Finance Digest Newsletter

persfin-digest@shore.net

This newsletter is open-ended to discussing personal finance matters. To subscribe, you must be careful to send an e-mail message to the appropriate address. The list of readers is maintained by a mailing list server, which means you must send a message to majordomo@shore.net with the text

subscribe persfin-digest

in the body of the message.

If you send your subscription message to the address at the beginning of this entry, every subscriber to the newsletter will see your message and you will not have even been added to the list!

When you want to ask a question or reply to somebody else's, send the e-mail message to persfin-digest@shore.net. Topics covered so far have ranged from comments about tax software to investment strategies like dollar cost averaging to how to calculate internal rate of return to how to set up a will for estate planning. The newsletter is moderated, so I have not seen a lot of the noise that one typically sees in newsgroups. This newsletter is mailed out to readers every day of the week.

Tax Digest

taxdigest@aol.com

The Tax Digest is an e-mail newsletter distributed by Gary Hoskins, MBA, CPA. He accurately describes the scope of the newsletter as providing income tax, business and estate planning, tax return preparation, asset protection planning, and consulting information. Subscribing to the newsletter is simple: just send an e-mail message to the address listed at the beginning of this entry. You don't need to include any text in the subject or body of the message. So far, the newsletter is being sponsored and distributed free of charge.

The newsletter has mentioned tax-related sites on the Internet such as the IRS Web page, contained news about events like the IRS's plan to hire 5,000 more auditors in 1995, and posted responses to a survey about tax software programs.

Taxing Times Web

http://www.scubed.com:8001/tax/tax.html

This Web area is much more developed than the IRS Web. You can find a diverse set of information here including forms, public-domain tax software, and pointers to a number of other Internet sites that have tax-related information. See Figure 2.5 for a sample of the Taxing Times Web site.

Taxing Times has copies of Federal and State income tax forms. It also has Revenue Canada Taxation forms, for our neighbors to the north. The Web provides a repository of tax software programs. They are easy to download; however, I sure would like to see a description of what each program does so that I could know in advance if I want to download it.

The best resource offered, however, is the entire Internal Revenue Service Code. Taxing Times provided the code, and a group at the MIT Lab for Computer Science put together a server that lets you get information on an

Figure 2.5:
This site carries all sorts of useful information for those of you who want to manage your taxes.

part of the IRS Tax Code. From within the Taxing Times home page, you simply select the *Tax Code* hypertext link and you will connect to MIT's server. You can then look at the Table of Contents to select a section of the code or use a search program to find the appropriate topic. If you have trouble accessing the Taxing Times Web page, the URL for the Tax Code is:

http://www.tns.lcs.mit.edu/uscode/

Portfolio Management

Most of the Internet sites covered in this section do not provide powerful portfolio management features, such as allocation reports by asset class or industry group. Nor can you generate performance reports for various time periods. Rather, these sites tend to provide information that allows you to make decisions about how you plan to allocate assets to achieve varying degrees of diversification and periodically get snapshot reports of your current holdings and what their total value is.

Modern Portfolio Management

http://www.magibox.net/~mpm

Matt Long, Vice President of Investments for Paine Webber, set up this site. He publishes a monthly newsletter, under the same name as this Web page, which describes his investment philosophy and management techniques. The newsletter focuses on current events and how they might impact the domestic stock and bond markets. The services available in this Web page are all free and open to the public.

You can download recent copies of the MPM newsletter. They need to be uncompressed first and are formatted in MS Word 6.0. Alternatively, you can send an e-mail message to mlong@magibox.net and include the text subscribe MPM newsletter to sign up to receive the newsletter via e-mail at the beginning of each new month.

In the past few monthly newsletters, Mr. Long has provided an analysis of the stock, bond, and currency markets. His analysis is international in scope and he presents useful insights to how the various markets' actions have an effect on each other. The newsletter is typically two to three pages in length and includes several charts.

The MPM Web page has an *Individual Investor Center* section that features several portfolio management services. One service is called the *Portfolio Allocation Review* (PAR). This service consists of a questionnaire that you fill out online. Your responses are analyzed and a printed report is then mailed to you via the U.S. Postal Service. The questionnaire asks for information about your investment portfolio (dollars in cash, fixed-income, stocks, and private), other net assets (house, car and valuables—less loans outstanding), current income and age and marginal tax bracket, expected short-term capital requirements (house renovations, education, etc.), and risk tolerance.

Another area in the Individual Investor Center, *Asset Allocations*, provides a general description of asset allocation structure based on risk tolerance/return objective. Three categories (conservative, moderate, and aggressive) are presented, with explanations of why a given asset allocation spectrum has been selected. For example, the conservative asset allocation is given a range of 100% in three-month Treasury bills for the most conservative investor, to 100% in the Lehman Corporate/Government Bond Index for the marginally conservative investor. A chart accompanies each of these areas and graphically displays the asset allocation range as a curve where the two axes measure return and risk relative to the S&P 500 index. You pick the point on the curve where the relative risk and return characteristics match your needs. Then find the closest marker number and look it up in a table below the chart. The table provides asset allocation mixes for each of the markers on the chart. One problem, currently, is that the graph goes off the right side of the page and you have no way to scroll right or resize the chart to see the entire graph.

Another area in the Individual Investor Center, Asset Allocations, provides a general description of asset allocation structure based on risk tolerance/ return objective.

Another service in the Individual Investor Center is the *Create a Fixed-Income Portfolio*. You can choose between a retirement/wealth building or an income generation goal for the portfolio. The section focuses your attention on return objective, time horizon, and credit quality (risk exposure). It contains good descriptions of what credit quality means with respect to fixed-income investments.

The MPM Web page also features some financial planning, stock analysis, and economic analysis areas. I discuss each of these areas in its respective section later in Part Two (for example, see the section on financial planning to find out what the MPM Web page has for that area).

PAWWS—Portfolio Accounting World-Wide from Security APL

http://pawws.secapl.com/

Security APL is an innovative investment organization that created a unique investment site on the Internet (see Figure 2.6). They started a site where people could get access to delayed quotes at no cost. Then they added a portfolio management program (PAWWS) that was introduced as a part of an investment game. This game still runs today; each contest lasts for one month and has a specific goal such as achieving the highest valued portfolio or the best risk/reward ratio. Individuals can register free of charge and participate in the game. Imaginary money is used as capital.

Security APL now offers a portfolio management and accounting service that individuals may subscribe to (for a fee) and use to track their various investments (you do not need to have an account with them in order to track

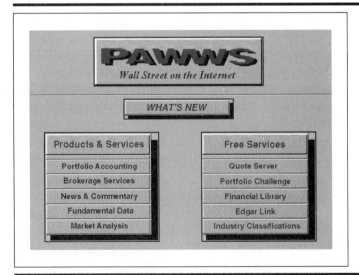

Figure 2.6:
Have you ever wanted to play the role of investment manager? This site lets you play in a free investment game and more.

your portfolio). The portfolio management service is called the SOURCE and costs $8.95 by the month, $25 by the quarter, or $95 by the year.

With the SOURCE, you can track up to 50 securities in multiple broker accounts. You start the portfolio by entering an initial figure for deposit of funds and an opening date.

This is NOT real money that you use in the portfolio (the fee is real, however). It is just a figure that you use as if you were setting up a portfolio in a software program on your own personal computer.

After setting up a portfolio with one or more sub-accounts containing cash, you can proceed to enter transactions. You are somewhat limited in terms of the transaction type and security. Valid transactions include open, close, receive, deliver, interest, dividend, and accrual. You can only buy a security to open—short sales do not work. In terms of securities, you can track money markets, U.S. and Canadian stocks, and mutual funds in a regular fashion. You do have the ability to create custom securities, primarily for investments like art, coins, and cars. However, the service is incapable of updating the values of custom securities—you must do that yourself.

The SOURCE provides portfolio reporting capabilities. You have four general types of reports available at your disposal:

Total Net Worth	This report displays holdings along with their cost, current price, current value, total gain/loss, and percent gain/loss. It also has totals for sub-accounts and the entire portfolio as a whole.
Schedule Of Gains/Losses	This report shows data on realized gains/losses. It lists purchase date and original cost, sale date and proceeds, and gain/loss.
Transaction History	This report shows, by sub-account, trades including the type, shares, date, price, amounts, and fees.
Asset Allocation Graph	This report is a pie chart that graphically depicts your portfolio by investment class.

The SOURCE also has the ability to process splits, name changes, mergers, and exchanges. The SOURCE provides more detailed portfolio management features than QuoteCom's portfolio management service (covered in the next entry), but QuoteCom's portfolio service covers more classes of securities (futures and options, for example) and you can enter short positions on QuoteCom too.

Security APL also offers access to a database containing fundamental stock information, and an online trading service (The Net Investor) that uses the SOURCE program to provide these portfolio management features along with a few additional ones. I discuss the fundamental data services offered by Security APL in the Fundamental Stock Analysis section later in Part Two, and I cover their Net Investor service in the Online Trading section.

QuoteCom

http://www.quote.com/

This is one of the most diverse and useful investment resources on the Internet today. It is no coincidence that most of the services QuoteCom offers cost money. QuoteCom does provide free, delayed stock quotes; however, you are limited to five quotes per day. Chris Cooper is responsible for setting up and running QuoteCom and he has done an excellent job.

QuoteCom offers several subscription services. The first option, logically, is called *Basic Service* and costs $9.95 per month. This service is, simply put, a great deal. You get several portfolio management features along with price data, company profiles, annual reports, ticker symbol searches, and news alerts, and end-of-day market summary and commentary.

This entry focuses on the portfolio management features of the basic service area; refer to the appropriate sections in Part Two of this book for more information about services relating to other investment categories (such as Fundamental Stock Analysis for company profiles and annual reports).

Basic service includes two portfolio management features: updates and alarm monitoring. You can construct a portfolio consisting of up to 50 securities. These securities may include stocks, mutual funds, futures, indexes, and Canadian stocks. It is extremely easy to manage a portfolio. You can add a security, delete a security, modify a security, or delete the portfolio. When entering transactions, you need to input the ticker

> *QuoteCom's Basic Service lets you construct a portfolio consisting of up to 50 securities.*

symbol, date of purchase, quantity of securities, transaction price, and (optionally) upper and lower alarm prices. You can sell a security short by entering a negative purchase quantity.

After creating a portfolio, you will receive a daily update via e-mail at the end of each day the market is open. You have six portfolio report formats to choose from:

◆ Valuation

◆ High/Low/Close/Change/Volume

◆ Close and Change

◆ ASCII Comma-Delimited

◆ Quicken and Spreadsheet

◆ Spreadsheet Valuation

The Valuation report displays (for each security) the quantity held, closing price, price change, dollar value, and change in dollar value. It also includes portfolio totals for dollar value and change in dollar value. The next two reports are pretty self-explanatory. The ASCII comma-delimited report includes data separated by commas (hence the term comma-delimited) and headers. Information in the report consists of ticker symbol, date, open, high, low, close, volume, and open interest (for futures). The data in this report can then be used by or stored in other programs. The Quicken and spreadsheet reports are also comma-delimited. The information includes tickers, dates, and price. You can then import this data to your Quicken or spreadsheet program. The Spreadsheet Valuation report contains the same data as the valuation report, but is in comma-delimited format with headers. You can also set the order by which securities are sorted in the report—by ticker symbol, exchange and ticker symbol, or date of acquisition.

When adding investments to your portfolio in QuoteCom, you can specify upper and lower price alarms. You will then receive an e-mail message during the day when the price of any security in your portfolio moves across the upper or lower alarm price.

These reports are nice and present timely information about a portfolio, but the Basic Service lacks some of the more useful features such as asset allocation and rate of return reporting. This might be something QuoteCom can add in the future. For now, you will have to use a full-fledged portfolio management program to handle the more detailed aspects of portfolio management analysis. I really like the convenience of receiving these updates via e-mail, however. This is a useful, cost-effective service that will benefit investors interested in monitoring the value of their investments.

Wall Street Software

http://www-bprc.mps.ohio-state.edu/cgi-bin/hpp?wsshome.html

This Web page is pretty basic and brief (see Figure 2.7). It consists of three parts: cross-links to other investment sites, software downloads, and an order/registration area.

The software download section has fewer than ten programs to choose from and all but two are demonstration (demo) programs. Each program is given a brief description and the size of the file is listed. The area has demos for three popular portfolio management programs:

◆ Captool

◆ Folioman

◆ Quant IX

There is also a downloader program that lets you retrieve prices from Prodigy to update the value of securities in Quicken. This site might develop into a much more useful resource once it adds further content. More demos and shareware and freeware, for example.

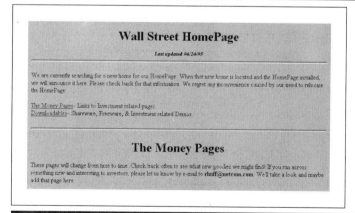

Figure 2.7:
If you like to try before you buy, this web site offers demo and shareware programs.

Fundamental Stock Analysis

This section deals with Internet sites that provide information that you can use when analyzing stocks based on their fundamentals. Fundamental screening is not quite available on the Internet yet, at least not at a cost-effective level for the individual investor. You should expect to see this type of service available in the second half of 1995, however. Several online vendors that offer fundamental screening services have announced plans to provide access via the Internet, but it is not clear how long it will take to make that type of service functionally available.

Most of the Internet sites covered in this section provide fundamental information on publicly listed companies, either in the form of full or condensed annual/quarterly reports or in the form of news stories detailing specific activities of a business as it relates to their fundamentals. Industry based information is also available. Companies are frequently compared to their siblings in the same industry when performing fundamental analysis.

Most of the Internet sites covered in this section provide fundamental information on publicly listed companies.

Some of this information is free, but this is the first section that really begins to include fee-based services. In some cases the fees are nominal, $10 to $20 per month. While this may seem expensive to some people, remember that it takes a lot of work to keep track of all this information. Frequently, the price is worth the timeliness and reliability of the information that you receive.

EDGAR/Internet Multicasting Service

mail@town.hall.org

town.hall.org

town.hall.org

http://town.hall.org/edgar/edgar.html

The Internet Multicasting Service (IMS) shown in Figure 2.8 works in conjunction with the Stern School of Business at New York University to research how SEC filings can be made easily accessible to the general public. The Stern School of Business also has an EDGAR (Electronic Data Gathering, Analysis, and Retrieval) site which is discussed in the following entry; however, it is a Web page—you can only access it with a Web browser. You can use the IMS's e-mail, FTP, and Gopher sites as alternative means of getting access to the EDGAR filings. I rate the Stern NYU Web page as a better interface than the IMS Web page because I think it is better organized and more

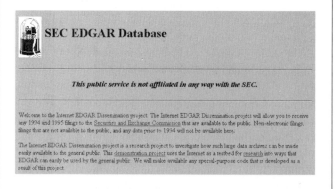

Figure 2.8: One of the two renowned EDGAR sites. Look here for free filings on publicly listed companies.

I rate the Stern NYU Web page as a better interface than the IMS Web page.

intuitive, but if you don't have access to a Web browser you have to go with the IMS sites.

If you want to get information about accessing IMS's EDGAR services via e-mail, send a message to mail@town.hall.org and include the text help in the body of the message. You can also use anonymous FTP to connect to IMS's FTP site. Connect to the site town.hall.org and go to the subdirectory /edgar where you will find some reference information files along with a number of subdirectories that contain various SEC filings. With Gopher, connect to town.hall.org, using port number 70. Because both EDGAR sites provide access to the same information, the content will be discussed only once under the next entry to avoid redundancy.

EDGAR/NYU Project

http://edgar.stern.nyu.edu/edgar.html

The previous entry introduced the IMS EDGAR (Electronic Data Gathering, Analysis, and Retrieval) sites which include access via e-mail, anonymous FTP, Gopher, and the World Wide Web. The IMS works on the EDGAR project in conjunction with the Stern School of Business at New York University. This NYU EDGAR site, shown in Figure 2.9, only provides World Wide Web access to the well-known SEC filings and is run by the EDGAR team at the Stern School. They received a grant from the NSF (remember them, the agency that created a major portion of the Internet's domestic infrastructure in the mid-1980s?) with the general goal "to enable wide dissemination and support all levels of user access to the corporate electronic filings submitted to the SEC."

As long as you have Web access to the Internet, this is a great site. The site contains electronic filings of certain publicly listed companies starting with data from the beginning of 1994. Not all publicly listed companies currently file electronically; however, all will be required to by mid-1996. Table 2.1 lays out the schedule for phasing in companies to start filing electronically. As you can see, well over six thousand companies should be filing electronically by the time this book is in print.

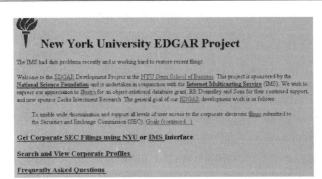

Figure 2.9:
The second of the two
EDGAR sites. This one
is managed by the
EDGAR project
administrators.

Table 2.1: SEC Phase-In Schedule for Electronic Form Filing

Group	Date	# of 1933 Act Companies	# of 1940 Act Companies	Cumulative
CF01	April 1993	240	250	490
CF02	July 1993	+753	+450	1,693
CF03	October 1993	+749	0	2,442
CF04	December 1993	+1,000	0	3,442
CF05	January 30, 1995	+1,499	+800	5,741
CF06	March 6, 1995	+1,497	+800	8,038
CF07	May 1, 1995	+1,499	+800	10,337
CF08	August 7, 1995	+1,496	0	11,833
CF09	November 6, 1995	+1,499	+800	14,132
CF10	May 6, 1996	+808	0	14,940
Totals		11,040	3,900	14,940

There are several dozen different types of forms that organizations and individuals file with the SEC. Some have little value or usefulness to the average person; others contain a wealth of detailed information about a company's business that you can't find in almost any other place. Form definitions are provided for many of the popular filings along with transcriptions of the Securities Acts of 1933 and 1940. The following are several examples of form definitions provided:

Form 10-K This is the annual report that most reporting companies file with the Commission. It provides a comprehensive overview of the registrant's business. The report must be filed within 90 days after the end of the company's fiscal year.

Form 10-Q Filed quarterly by most registered companies. It includes unaudited financial statements and provides a continuing view of the company's financial position during the year. The report must be filed for each of the first three fiscal quarters and is due within 45 days of the close of the quarter.

Schedule 13-D Discloses beneficial ownership of certain registered equity securities. Any person or group of persons who acquires a beneficial ownership of more than 5% of a class of registered equity securities of certain issuers must file a Schedule 13-D reporting such acquisition. Moreover, any material changes in the facts set forth in the Schedule precipitate a duty to promptly file an amendment. The SEC's rules define the term "beneficial owner" to be any person who directly or indirectly shares voting power or investment power (the power to sell the security).

Schedule 14B In the event that there is a proxy contest with respect to the election or removal of a company's directors, any "participant" in such contest must file a Schedule 14B. As a general rule participants other than the issuer must file Schedule 14B's at least five business days prior to making any solicitation, whereas the issuer's participants must file within five business days after the opposition solicitation has begun.

Now that you have a taste of the kind of filings available from the EDGAR project, you might ask, "How can I find a certain filing?" The NYU EDGAR team has done an excellent job setting up their Web page to provide users with an intuitive interface. Most of the relevant features are located under the *Get Corporate SEC Filings* hypertext menu of the Web's home page. You have about a half dozen different ways to search for various filings, and they all center around selecting a date range of interest

> *You have about a half dozen different ways to search for various filings, and they all center around selecting a date range of interest..., security name..., and type of form(s) desired.*

(for example, last week or last month), security name (a partial name is acceptable), and type of form(s) desired. For those who know what they want specifically, the *Fast Retrieval* menu will yield the quickest route to getting the desired set of files. A search will result in a response that lists the matches. These matches are in hypertext format so that you can automatically select and view a particular filing.

The *Retrieve from Universe* menu provides the most open-ended search engine. This is especially useful for newcomers because of its ease of use. You have three scroll boxes that list the choices for date ranges, type of form filing, and—best of all—a full-length listing of all securities' full names sorted in alphabetical order. A noteworthy feature of this search engine is that you have the ability to select multiple companies and forms, which reduces the amount of time spent rerunning searches.

For those of you who want to see all the filings for a particular type of form for a specific time period, you will want to use the *Form Only Lookup* menu. Just like it sounds, you pick one or more types of filing forms and a recent period of time to see all the companies that have filed those forms during that time. For example, this would fit the bill if you wanted to see all of the quarterly reports filed in the last week.

Along a similar vein, you can select the *Current Filing Analysis* menu to look at reports filed over the past one to five business days. And for those interested in following who owns large stakes in public companies, the *Schedule 13D Acquisition Reporting* menu will let you search by company name and date range.

If you have trouble locating a company or want to find out when it is supposed to begin filing electronically, select the *CIK and SIC Utilities* menu on the Web's home page. One search engine allows you to enter a company's partial or full name. It will return any matches along with CIK number, phase-in code, and phase-in date. Another search engine provides somewhat useful search capabilities of SIC (Security Industry Code) industry groupings. With this engine, you can search for a company by name (partial) to get its SIC number and description, or search for the companies in an SIC group either by SIC number and description or by a word in the SIC description. I found the classification system to have some weak points, however. For example, when I selected the SIC group *#1040-Gold and Silver Ores* and submitted the request, the system returned the following list of companies (notice how the long names were truncated):

Battle Mountain Gold

Campbell Resources I

Canyon Resources Cor

Hecla Mining Co

Kinross Gold Corp

Mk Gold Co

Morrison Knudsen Cor

Newmont Gold Co

This list did not include Placer Dome Gold which I knew to belong in this group. Then I ran the search for companies with a name matching "Placer," which returned Placer Dome Gold. I submitted that company to see its SIC number and description. The system returned several listings including Gold and Silver Ores. The point of this is that while you can use this feature as a useful source of information, do not rely upon it as a comprehensive and authoritative source of industry grouping information.

The NYU EDGAR Web also has an FAQ menu on its home page. The FAQ list includes a number of pertinent concerns relating to how one can get more use from the resources provided. The Web has a Coming Soon menu to inform users of future developments. Upcoming additions include a company profile feature and an Intro To EDGAR For Beginners area.

misc.invest.stocks

misc.invest.stocks

This newsgroup gets a large number of daily postings, usually around one hundred. It is very similar to the misc.invest newsgroup; in fact a number of messages are frequently cross-posted to both newsgroups. As the name implies, the focus of discussion in this newsgroup is stocks. Actually, the quality of posting here is pretty good in a general sense. You should not expect to receive responses from financial analysts, although you occasionally see some well-informed and experienced input. Most of the time the discussions take place among a wide range of individuals sharing tidbits of information and, more often, opinions about a company's prospects based on personal experiences. This is an interesting area to keep up with if you follow stocks, but you should get reliable data from a second source before acting on any information obtained in this newsgroup.

Modern Portfolio Management

http://www.magibox.net/~mpm

I discuss this page primarily in the Portfolio Management section earlier in Part Two. However, it provides some resources for other areas of investing, including fundamental stock analysis. The services available from this Web page are all free.

The MPM Web page has a *Research Center* area that provides information about stocks. This center features Paine Webber's Focus Stock List. The list covers close to 30 stocks and divides them into three classes: aggressive, growth, and income. The focus list gives a brief summary of ratings, price, and earnings estimates; however, the really nice feature of this focus list is the hypertext links to individual reports on each stock. When you select any stock that appears in the list, you get to see a detailed research report on that company (prepared by Paine Webber). The research reports contain some more fundamental data about historical quarterly earnings, beta, and so on. The reports also have detailed information about the company's line of business and the issues currently of importance. This is a great area to check out.

The Research Center also provides a list of weekly earnings announcements and their estimates. The list covers approximately a dozen stocks each week and includes such information as:

◆ Paine Webber's rating of the stock

◆ Estimated report date

◆ Paine Webber's earnings estimate

◆ Consensus earnings estimates

◆ Actual earnings, if already released

You can view the latest five lists. From the home page, select the *Free Subscription Services* area. Select the hypertext link named *View a Brief History of EPS Announcements*.

You can subscribe to receive a free weekly update of the earnings estimate list. Simply send an e-mail message to mlong@magibox.net and include the text subscribe EPS in the body of the message.

PAWWS—Portfolio Accounting World-Wide from Security APL

http://pawws.secapl.com/

Security APL created and manages this Web page and its services. I present more background information about this area in the Portfolio Management section earlier in Part Two.

Some of the Web's services are free and others cost money. Two areas in this Web offer resources useful to the fundamental analysis of stocks.

The first area, *Industry Classifications*, appears under *Free Services*. It divides stocks into 88 separate categories. Select any category to view the stocks in that industry. Stocks are ranked by market capitalization, and their beta is also listed. Each stock has a hypertext link to its corresponding reports on the EDGAR Internet site as well.

The second area, data from *Ford Investor Services, Inc.*, is available to subscribers of the SOURCE, a PAWWS portfolio management service. Ford Investor Services, Inc. is a financial information service that maintains a database of fundamental data on over 2,600 publicly listed companies. You can subscribe to one of three levels of service here:

Level One	13 data fields	$10 per month
Level Two	27 data fields	$16 per month
Level Three	42 data fields	$20 per month

Compared to diskette-based fundamental databases that also provide screening capabilities, this is a relatively expensive feature. There is no indication that you can perform fundamental screening with any of these levels of service. Level Three appears to be comparable to the S&P Stock Guide service offered by QuoteCom, which is discussed in the next entry.

QuoteCom

E-mail to services@quote.com

ftp.quote.com

quote.com

http://www.quote.com/

QuoteCom is first mentioned under the Portfolio Management section earlier in Part Two. This section covers most of QuoteCom's various services. QuoteCom is one of the best investment sites on the Internet today. See Figure 2.10 for the QuoteCom home page. Unfortunately, the bulk of the services are not free. On the good side, you can select which services you want and each service is reasonably priced considering what you get. General services that you can subscribe to include:

Basic	$9.95 per month
Chart	$9.95 per month
S&P MarketScope Alerts	$14.95 per month
S&P Stock Guide	$24.95 per month
BusinessWire Reports	$9.95 per month
PR Newswire Reports	$9.95 per month
S&P News Reports	$12.95 per month
Canadian Stocks and Commodities	$9.95 per month
Overseas Stocks and Commodities	$19.95 per month
Freese-Notis Weather Forecasts	$19.95 per month

Basic Services   The Basic Services are a great deal at $9.95 per month. You get access to delayed quotes for securities on domestic exchanges, portfolio

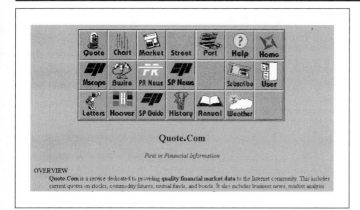

Figure 2.10
Check out one of the
most robust and infor-
mative investment
sites on the Internet
today, here at
QuoteCom.

management updates (covered in the Portfolio Management section of Part
Two in this book), end-of-day update files (covered in the Technical Analysis
and News sections of Part Two), Hoover company profiles, annual reports on
certain publicly listed companies, and ticker symbol search capabilities.

You can get up to 100 delayed quotes for securities listed on U.S.
exchanges. You can use e-mail, FTP, Telnet, or the Web via the addresses
listed at the beginning of this entry to access these quotes. Securities accessible include stocks, mutual funds, and futures. A quote includes the following information:

◆ Name

◆ Ticker symbol

◆ Open, high, low, close, volume

◆ Bid and ask prices

◆ Earnings per share for the latest 12 months

◆ Price-to-earnings ratio

◆ Dividend

◆ 52-week high and low prices

Hoover Company Profiles are compiled by an organization called Reference, Inc. and are available as a part of QuoteCom's Basic Services or at a cost of $2.95 per report for nonsubscribers. There are five types of profiles that you can get:

◆ Public Company

◆ Private Company

◆ Emerging Growth Companies

◆ Industry Profiles

◆ Worldwide Companies

The Emerging Growth Companies profile actually contains information that also exists in the Public and Private Company areas. You have over 1,000 public companies and 200 industry profiles from which to choose. I could not find specific numbers for the other types of profiles.

A profile contains such information as an overview of the company and its line(s) of business, a list of important people who are responsible for managing the company, address and phone number contact information, a list of key competitors, and a financial summary of data from income and balance sheet statements. You will also find historical fundamental data going back approximately five years. If you want basic information about earnings, sales, return on equity, current ratio, and market capitalization, for example, you will find it here. However, you are not likely to get such detailed data as depreciation, cost of goods sold, or free cash flow.

If you want basic information about earnings, sales, return on equity, current ratio, and market capitalization, you will find it here.

Basic Service also includes access to annual report information. Unfortunately, the information is not directly accessible from QuoteCom—you submit a request for the particular company and the annual report is mailed from the East Coast within the next two business days. You can request up to 20 reports per day. These reports will only be mailed to U.S. postal mailing addresses. You will also receive two issues of the Security Traders Handbook. This service is handled by Bay Tact Corp. and not directly by QuoteCom.

Chart Service See the section on technical analysis in Part Two for a description of this service.

S&P MarketScope Alerts This service provides more information, covering virtually all areas of investing. It is a bit more expensive than the Basic Service, costing $14.95 a month. If you plan to manage your investments actively, this service provides you with timely information about stocks and more. It has company and industry profiles and analyses, earnings estimates and dividend forecasts, and daily market commentaries. You are limited to 50 requests a day, but this should be more than sufficient for all but the professional investor.

The service has *STARS* and a number of diverse reports. STARS stands for STock Appreciation Ranking System. Standard and Poor's rates about 1,000 stocks based on their expected future performance on a scale of 1 to 5. The diverse reports consist of 24 articles that are updated with varying frequency (see Table 2.2 for a listing). QuoteCom keeps the latest 90 days of data as well, which you can access via FTP. To cover this data in depth would take more space than is appropriate for this book. If you actively use this service, it can be well worth the price.

S&P Stock Guide This service focuses exclusively on stocks. It is also fairly expensive, weighing in at $24.95 a month. Given the high cost, you might

Table 2.2: S&P MarketScope Reports Available from QuoteCom

Market Commentary	Stock Allocation Model
Today's Headlines	Investment Strategy
Touted on TV	Economic Calendar/Forecast
Touted in the Media	Economy Watch Indicators
Today's Perspectives	MoneyScope
Stock Splits	Today's Interest Rates
Technical Market Indicators	Today's Exchange Rates
Takeover Talk (by company)	Treasury Market Commentary
Takeover Talk (by date)	Currency Market Commentary
Stock of the Week	New Earnings Estimates
Monthly Economic Commentary	New Issues: Calendar
Special Studies	New Issues: Recent Performance

want to weigh its benefits against the similar services offered by diskette-based fundamental stock screening packages. While this service does not currently have screening capabilities, they are supposed to be added soon. The major considerations here include frequency of data updates, number of securities covered, and the depth of fundamental data provided.

This service is updated daily. It covers over 5,900 common and preferred stocks listed on the NYSE, AMEX, and NASDAQ exchanges. You are limited to a maximum of 25 reports a day. The information included in each report is listed in Table 2.3.

Table 2.3: Data Included in the S&P Stock Guide Reports	
Company Name	Latest Dividend
Ticker Symbol	Indicated Annual Dividend
CUSIP Number	Pay Date for Latest Dividend
S&P 500 Indicator	Ex-Dividend Date for Latest Dividend
S&P Earnings and Dividend Ranking	Earnings for the Latest 12 Months
Option Ticker Symbol	5-Year Compounded Annual Earnings Growth Rate
Amount of Shares Held by Institutions	Interim Earnings
STAR Rating	Interim Earnings Period
Beta	Reference Year for Actual and Estimated Earnings
Current Assets	
Current Liabilities	Current Year's Earnings
Date of Balance Sheet Report	Next Year's Earnings Estimate
Long-Term Debt	Earnings Footnotes
Number of Shares of Common Stock Outstanding	Month in which Fiscal Year Ends
Number of Shares of Preferred Stock Outstanding	High and Low Price Ranges for Each of the Last 4 Years
Balance Sheet Footnotes	Dividends for Each of the Last 4 Years
Price-to-Earnings Ratio Based on Latest 12 Months' Earnings	Earnings for Each of the Last 4 Years
Average Daily Volume for the Latest 30 Trading Days	Equity per Share for Each of the Last 4 Years
	Revenues per Share for Each of the Last 4 Years
52-Week High and Low Prices	Net Income per Share for Each of the Last 4 Years
Calendar Year High and Low Prices	
Dividend Yield	Most Recent Split Date and Divisor

BusinessWire Reports This is a news reporting service, and a fairly affordable one at that. It costs $9.95 per month to subscribe to BusinessWire. The service primarily carries news releases. You can use this or PR Newswire, mentioned next, to keep up with news about stocks. These services overlap to a large extent, but each does get some news releases that the other does not.

You are limited to a maximum of 25 reports per day with BusinessWire. Data is updated daily; however, QuoteCom keeps the last 90 days of news releases. If you also get the Basic Service, then you will receive a message in your portfolio update about any news on securities in the portfolio. You can search through news by day, by ticker symbol, or by category. There are about forty categories to choose from. See Table 2.4.

Table 2.4: Search Categories for BusinessWire

Earnings Reports	Environment (including recycling, waste)
Dividend Reports	Food and Beverage
Advisory Reports	Forest Products
Product Announcements	Government
Management Changes	Insurance
Mergers and Acquisitions	Manufacturing
Reminders of Upcoming Events	Medicine (including healthcare)
Aerospace and Defense	Mining
Apparel and Textiles	Oil and Gas
Automotive	Pharmaceuticals
Banking (includes financial services)	Real Estate
Biotechnology	Restaurants
Building and Construction	Retail
Chemicals and Plastics	Sports
High Technology Companies	Supermarkets
Computers and Electronics	Telecommunications
Education	Travel and Airlines
Energy	Transportation
Entertainment	Utilities
Environmental Copy	

PR Newswire Reports The PR Newswire Reports are similar to what the BusinessWire Reports offer. Many of the details are the same: the cost is $9.95 per month, data is updated daily, and QuoteCom keeps the latest 90 days of reports. One nice difference is that you are limited to a maximum of 50 reports per day, instead of 25 as is the case with the BusinessWire service. You can search for news releases by ticker symbol, day, or category. Categories are divided into 30 industry groups and 23 subjects. Table 2.5 lists these categories.

S&P News Reports QuoteCom offers yet a third news service, S&P News Reports. It is a bit more expensive than either of the other two, costing $12.95 a month. You can retrieve up to a maximum of 50 reports per day, and QuoteCom keeps the latest 90 days of news releases. If you get the basic service, you also receive automatic updates for any news items about securities in your portfolio.

This news service is a bit more focused toward the fundamental side than the other two. The news service covers approximately 6,500 publicly listed securities. You can search for reports by ticker symbol, day, or category. There are 49 different categories to choose from. See Table 2.6 for a listing.

Table 2.5: PR Newswire News Release Categories

Advertising	Tobacco
Aerospace and Defense	Transportation, Trucking, and Railroads
Agriculture	Utilities
Airlines and Aviation	Accounting News and Issues
Automotive	Acquisitions, Mergers, and Takeovers
Banking and Financial Services	Bankruptcy
Chemicals	Bond and Stock Ratings
Computers and Electronics	Contracts
Construction and Building	Political Campaigns
Entertainment	Dividends
Environmental	Earnings
Food and Beverage	Economic News, Trends, and Analysis
Gambling and Casinos	Federal and State Legislation
Healthcare and Hospitals	Government news
Household, Consumer, and Cosmetic Products	Financing Agreements

Table 2.5: PR Newswire News Release Categories (continued)

Insurance	Joint Ventures
Leisure, Travel, Hotels, and Restaurants	Licensing Agreements
Machinery	New Products and Services
Maritime and Shipbuilding	Offerings
Mining and Metals	Oil and Gas Discoveries
Medical Sciences and Pharmaceuticals	Personnel Announcements
Oil and Energy	Real Estate Transactions
Paper, Forest Products, and Containers	Restructurings and Recapitalizations
Publishing and Information Services	Shareholder Rights Plans
Retail	Sales Reports
Telecommunications	Labor
Textiles	

Table 2.6: S&P News Reports Search Categories

Annual Earnings	Financing (credit)
Annual Reports	Going Private
Initial Public Offerings (IPO's)	Licensing and Marketing Agreements
Interim Earnings	Leveraged Buoyouts
Interim Reports	Lines of Business Resources
New Products	Liquidation
Mergers and Acquisitions	Litigation
S&P Ratings	Management's Discussion
Stock Buybacks	Management Changes
Contracts	Operational Statistics
S&P Index Changes	Pro Forma Reports
Tender Offers	Qualified Institutional Buyers
Securities Offerings	Redemptions
Name Changes	Registrations
Performance Estimates	Rights Offerings
Financing (private placements)	Retail Sales
Backlog	Securities Descriptions and Interests
Business Failures	Spinoffs
Debt Offerings	Securities Trading Data

Table 2.6: S&P News Reports Search Categories (continued)	
Changes in Charter	Utility Rate Changes
Change of Control	Exchange Rate Offers
Company Descriptions	Airline Traffic Estimates
Corporate Restructuring	Auto Sales and Production Statistics
Capital Spending Plans	Miscellaneous
Dividend Changes, Stock Distributions	

Telescan

http://www.telescan.com/

Telescan is an online service that focuses on finance and investing. I cover it in both the Technical Analysis section and the News, Quotes, and Market Statistics sections of Part Two. Telescan has recently begun construction and development of an Internet site that will offer the same kinds of services that are currently available through direct telephone connections. The programs and services that they offer will be primarily fee based; however, some will be free.

It is quite likely that the Internet site, once completed, will include several fundamental analysis services such as screening programs and news services. You will probably be able to get Zacks Earning Estimates, S&P MarketGuide Reports, and SEC Online Reports.

Wall Street Direct

http://www.cts.com:80/~wallst/

Wall Street Direct is discussed primarily in the Technical Analysis section of Part Two. It has one area that directly pertains to fundamental stock analysis—the online bookstore. Located under *Products and Services*, this bookstore lists books based on category. The fundamental stock category lists close to 30 books. It contains a number of classic texts and lengthy reference books. I recommend this area to individuals who want to find out where they can learn more about this subject.

Fixed-Income Analysis

This section covers the Internet sites that provide information useful in evaluating fixed income securities. Most of the sites simply provide current and historical interest rate figures for the banking system (for example, Federal Funds and Prime) and for securities (for example, Treasury bills and Corporate Bonds).

FRED—Federal Reserve Economic Data

(314) 621-1824

The Federal Reserve Bank of St. Louis currently operates FRED as a bulletin board service, which means that you can only access it by dialing their BBS directly; however, they are looking into providing access via the Internet. This is the only service in the book that does not currently offer access via the Internet, but I included it for two reasons. First, the data offered is very useful. Second, given the way the Internet is growing, I find it hard to believe that this service would not offer Internet access in the near future.

Even though it is a long-distance phone call for most individuals, I recommend that you call them first at (314) 444-8562 and inquire as to the existence of Internet access. If they still don't have an Internet site, you'll have to dial in to the BBS using the number listed at the head of this section to take a look at their data. Connection setup is the standard no parity, 8-bit data length, 1 stop bit, and full duplex. They support baud rates up to 14,400 bps.

FRED provides current and historical economic/financial data. The primary value of FRED is the ability to download historical files and update files. Files are currently organized in 28 separate directories, as follows:

◆ Historical Daily/Weekly U.S. Financial Data

◆ Historical Data—Monetary Aggregates

◆ Historical Data—Interest Rates

◆ Historical Data—Reserves

◆ Historical Data—Loans

◆ Business/Fiscal Data

◆ Gross Domestic Product and Components

◆ Consumer Price Index

◆ Producer Price Index

◆ Employment and Population Figures

◆ St. Louis REVIEW Data

◆ International Data

◆ Regional Business Indicators

◆ Federal Reserve Statistical Releases

◆ Master File

◆ Update Files—Monetary Aggregates

◆ Update Files—Interest Rates

◆ Update Files—Reserves

◆ Update Files—Loans

◆ Update Files—Business/Fiscal

◆ Update Files—U.S. Financial Data

◆ Update Files—Gross Domestic Product

◆ Update Files—Consumer Price Index

◆ Update Files—Producer Price Index

◆ Update Files—Employment and Population

◆ Update Files—International Data

◆ Update Files—Regional Business Indicators

◆ Community Affairs Department Profiles

Half of these directories contain historical data that goes back at least several decades, and sometimes to the beginning of the century. The information is concisely presented and easy to download. A few examples will help to illustrate the kinds of data available. The *Historical Daily/Weekly U.S. Financial Data* directory includes files with such data as Federal Funds rate averages from 1966 to present, the 1-year Treasury Bill rate on the secondary market from 1974 to present, the Corporate AAA Bond rate from 1965 to present, and the average 90-day CD rate from 1969 to present. The *Historical Data— Monetary Aggregates* directory has monthly data on the Federal Funds rate from 1954 to present, the Discount rate from 1914 to present, and the average Corporate AAA and BAA Bond rates from 1919 to present. These are just but a few of the many files available. This site also has a wealth of economic data, which I discuss in the Economic Analysis section later in Part Two.

Gruntal & Company—Weekly Market Summary

http://www.gruntal.com/investments/wms.html

Gruntal & Company offers summary market information through their Web page. Because most of the information consists of market statistics, I cover this Web site more fully in the News, Quotes, and Market Statistics section later in Part Two. The site provides some brief information relating to money rates that can be of use to individuals analyzing fixed-income securities.

One of the menus on the home page is *Money Rates*. By selecting this menu, you can obtain rates for the current week and previous week. These rates include:

◆ Discount

◆ Prime

◆ Federal Funds

◆ Broker Call

◆ 6-Month CD

◆ 2-, 5-, 10-, and 30-Year Treasury Instruments

The Holt Reports, covered in the next entry, provide current rates for a broader range of securities; however, Gruntal & Company provides a sense of how these rates have changed over the past week.

Holt's Market Report

geoholt@netcom.com

misc.invest

ftp.netcom.com

wuecon.wustl.edu

http://turnpike.net/metro/holt/index.html

I discuss the Holt Reports at length in the News, Quotes, and Market Statistics section later in Part Two. Refer to that section to get detailed information about accessing the reports. The reports are generated for each trading day. One of the four reports, *Holt's Market Report*, contains updates for a range of interest rates that can be useful when analyzing bonds. At the end of the Market Report, you can find details on the current rates for the Federal Funds rate, the Prime rate, 3- and 6-month Treasury Bills, 1-, 3-, 5-, and 10-year Treasury Notes, and 30-year Treasury Bonds. The report lists the latest rate, the change, and the previous trading day's rate.

Ohio State University Finance Department

http://www.ohio-state.edu/dept/fin/osudata.html

This site has a limited amount of useful information. Much of it is incomplete; however, it does have some information pertaining to fixed-income investments. You can find Treasury Bond futures price tick data for the past year and information about corporate debt issues between 1983 and 1993. In addition, there is some very "historic" information on interest rates—specifically for France back in the 1700s. Not very useful today, but sort of interesting.

QuoteCom

ftp.quote.com

http://www.quote.com/

QuoteCom is first mentioned under the Portfolio Management section in Part Two of this book, and most of QuoteCom's services are covered in another section of Part Two (Fundamental Stock Analysis); this section focuses on the *Street Pricing* service that QuoteCom offers.

Street Pricing costs $9.95 per month (in addition to the QuoteCom Basic Service) and provides quotes on U.S. Treasury and government agency securities. You are limited to a maximum of 50 quotes a day, and you can add them to your portfolio. Bear Stearns, who functions as a primary dealer in those markets, is the source of the quotes. You can get real-time quotes on over 500 debt securities with different

> *QuoteCom's Street Pricing service gives you real-time quotes on over 500 debt securities with different maturities and coupons.*

maturities and coupons. The following is a list of some of the categories of debt securities included.

◆ 3-, 6-, and 12-Month Treasury Bills

◆ 1-, 2-, 3-, 5-, 7-, 10-, and 30-Year Treasury Notes and Bonds

◆ 30-, 60-, 90-, and 180-Day Certificates of Deposit

◆ 30-, 60-, 90-, and 180-Day Commercial Paper

◆ 30-, 60-, 90-, and 180-Day Bankers Acceptance

◆ Overnight, 30-, 60-, 90-, and 180-Day LIBOR

◆ Prime Rate

◆ FFCB (Federal Farm Credit Banks)

◆ FHLB (Federal Home Loan Banks)

◆ FHLM (Federal Home Loan Mortgage Corporation)

◆ FNMA (Federal National Mortgage Association)

◆ GNMA (Government National Mortgage Association)

◆ RFC (Resolution Funding Corp)

T-Bill Direct

http://www.netfactory.com/mondenet/tbdira1.html

J.W. Korth and Company bring you this Internet Web page shown in Figure 2.11. They offer Treasury instrument brokerage services to the individual investor at competitive rates. This Web page only provides background information regarding Treasury securities; you are not able to place orders through this site. J.W. Korth and Company allows individuals to buy Treasury securities on the primary market and to trade previously issued Treasury instruments on secondary markets.

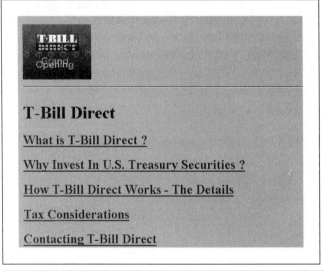

Figure 2.11:
Did you ever want to know how to buy and sell Treasury Bills, Notes, and Bonds as an individual? Look here to learn more.

The primary market is where the Treasury holds an auction to sell its Bills, Notes, and Bonds. Few individuals bought securities directly from the Treasury until recently; this was generally considered in the domain of the professional and institutional investor. The Treasury developed a service to simplify the process for individuals. This service is called *Treasury Direct*, and it allows individuals to purchase Treasury securities directly without having to pay any commissions. J.W. Korth and Company provide a service of their own called *T-Bill Direct*, which handles all of the paperwork involved in purchasing Treasury securities through Treasury Direct. In return, they charge a fee that is less than normal brokerage commissions. Remember that these two services are separate and not directly related to each other.

> *Treasury Direct...allows individuals to purchase Treasury securities directly without having to pay any commissions.*

If you are interested in learning more about Treasury Direct (and T-Bill Direct), this site should be able to answer all of your questions. It provides an FAQ list that answers many questions about the mechanics and the advantages of using Treasury Direct. The Web page also has a glossary that provides brief definitions of common fixed-income terms such as basis point, current yield, and tender. The explanations are clear and concise.

Wall Street Direct

http://www.cts.com:80/~wallst/

I discuss Wall Street Direct primarily in the Technical Analysis section later in Part Two. It has one area that directly pertains to the analysis of fixed-income securities—the online bookstore. Located under *Products and Services*, this bookstore lists books based on category. The first category in the bookstore is *Bonds*. This is a good place to visit if you are looking to learn more about analyzing fixed-income securities.

Mutual Fund Analysis

This section includes those sites that provide information about investing in mutual funds. The sites covered in this section provide a diversity of information. Some contain the detailed information about one or more funds' background, others provide an interactive forum for discussion, and one provides reference lists and software reviews on mutual fund books and programs.

EDGAR/NYU Project

http://edgar.stern.nyu.edu/edgar.html

This site only provides World Wide Web access to the EDGAR (Electronic Data Gathering, Analysis, and Retrieval) files. I cover the NYU EDGAR site and its sibling EDGAR/IMS site in detail in the Fundamental Analysis section earlier in Part Two. Refer to those entries for background information about the EDGAR project and its other resources. The two sites share access to the same set of resources; however, the IMS site also provides access via e-mail, anonymous FTP, and Gopher in addition to the World Wide Web.

Although several areas in the Web page offer information relating to mutual fund filings, I found little in the way of useful information. The *Ge Corporate SEC Filings* area has *Mutual Fund Retrieval* and *Prospectu: Search* menus. The Mutual Fund Retrieval menu lets you search for mutua fund filings within a selected time period; however, you can only specify form type and date range. The Prospectus Search lets you look for funds' filings b fund name and time period. You have the ability to enter the first few letter: of a fund's name (usually three letters are sufficient). The search returns ; list of matching funds' filings, which appear with hypertext links, which wil be nice if they can maintain them; unfortunately, I always got an "Unable to Locate File" error message upon selecting a link.

You can also get CIK (Central Index Key) and phase-in date information from the *CIK and SIC Utilities* menu on the home page. I did not find the information on mutual funds to be anywhere near as useful as the information available on publicly listed equity securities throughout the entire site.

Fidelity Investments Information Center

http://www.fid-inv.com/

Fidelity has its own Web page shown in Figure 2.12. This is a fairly recent development, having been announced in early 1995. Consequently, this page offers less information than some other Internet sites with information on mutual funds. And this page, obviously, focuses on Fidelity's own mutual funds and brokerage services.

Out of six areas, two have the most useful information and services for the investor. The *Mutual Funds* area details a wealth of information on about 150 of Fidelity's mutual funds. The funds are classified into 4 main groups and they are further divided into 13 detailed groups (see Table 2.7).

Figure 2.12:
Visit this Web site to learn more about mutual funds and one of the leaders in the industry.

Table 2.7: Mutual Fund Groupings for Fidelity's Web Page

Money Markets	Money Market
	Federal Tax-Free Money Market
	State Tax-Free Money Market
Income	Government
	Corporate
	Global
	Federal Tax-Free Bonds
	State Tax-Free Bonds
Growth	Growth
	Growth and Income
	International
	Select Portfolios
Asset Allocation	Asset Allocation

Each mutual fund has hypertext links that, when selected, bring detailed information about the fund, including the following categories:

◆ Ticker Symbol

◆ CUSIP Number

◆ Wall Street Journal Symbol

◆ Inception Date

◆ Sales Charge

◆ Redemption Fee

◆ Minimum Initial Investment

◆ Minimum Initial IRA Investment

◆ Minimum Initial College UGMA Investment

◆ Lipper Ranking

◆ Fund Description

◆ 1-, 5-, and 10-Year Average Returns

◆ Portfolio Manager

Return calculations include reinvestment of dividend and capital gains distributions, and any fees or charges. You can view a chart showing how an investment of $10,000 would have performed over the past ten years (starting upon either the date ten years ago or the inception date of the fund, whichever is more recent). And you can view a chart showing the recent monthly NAV history for a given fund. If you wish to obtain further information on a fund, you may select it and request that its prospectus be mailed to your U.S. postal mailing address.

Another useful area in Fidelity's Web page is called *Investor Tools*. This area has six different features. Several of these features simply make reference to Fidelity publications that their customers and subscribers receive, but the other features provide mutual fund and financial planning information (refer to the Personal Financial Planning section earlier in Part Two of this book for details on the financial planning features).

> *The FundMatch questionnaire is well written and gets you to think about a number of basic investment planning issues.*

The first feature listed is the *Fidelity FundMatch* service. You fill out a questionnaire that asks questions about your investment profile (return objective, risk tolerance, and time horizon) and submit it. Then FundMatch returns a score and presents you with a list of mutual fund groups that meet these criteria. The questionnaire is well written and gets you to think about a number of basic investment planning issues.

Another feature lists definitions and descriptions for three general mutual fund categories—money market, income, and growth. While brief, the information will be useful to beginners unfamiliar with the basic characteristics of mutual funds.

misc.invest.funds

misc.invest.funds

This newsgroup belongs to the family of misc.invest newsgroups and covers the topic of investing in mutual funds. Misc.invest.funds has a moderate volume of postings, averaging over fifty messages a day. This newsgroup has good content—it lacks a lot of the garbage that you find in many newsgroups.

You will find that readers frequently discuss the differences between several similar mutual funds. For example, I found a comparison of three

Asian mutual funds, one of which invests its capital evenly across several countries' markets including Japan; the second invests its capital in several countries' markets, but excludes Japan completely; and the third invests virtually all of its capital in the Japanese market.

Individuals discuss many other topics, including mutual funds in 401(k) plans, brokerage houses that provide mutual fund based services, the differences between funds that have loads and those without loads, the effects that 12B-1 charges have on return over long periods of time, and of course the performance of various funds. This is a good resource if you invest in mutual funds.

NETworth

http://networth.galt.com:80/

Two enterprising, and energetic, gentlemen have done an excellent job in establishing a resource (Figure 2.13) on the Internet where individuals can get free access to a wealth of information on over 5,000 mutual funds and order more materials, such as a prospectus, to be delivered via the U.S. Postal Service. To access the most useful areas, you will need to register (at no cost). This simply consists of entering your name, U.S. mailing address, e-mail address, and selecting a password.

Figure 2.13:
This site offers valuable information on thousands of mutual funds, and it's all free.

In the past, mutual funds were required to mail their materials to prospective investors before allowing them to invest; however, current trends are leading toward changes that will allow these materials to be delivered via e-mail. This could benefit individuals in several ways. First, response time would be greatly improved—the individual would not have to wait a week or more, materials could be downloaded instantaneously. Second, mutual funds might be able to spend less money to advertise their services, thereby reducing expenses charged to investor's capital.

Although NETworth has several interesting areas in their Web page, the main area of value is their *Mutual Fund Market Manager*. You can access this area from NETworth's main menu. This area is split into three levels, but as to why, I am not exactly sure—all three levels feature similar information relating to mutual funds. Be that as it may, you can get a wealth of information from all three levels.

Level One contains a fund search utility, NAV (Net Asset Value) quotes, the 100% No-Load Mutual Fund Council, and a number of mutual fund family sections. The fund search utility is probably the best part of all of NETworth. You can search for an individual mutual fund by ticker symbol, or for multiple mutual funds based on a string search (using part of a name) such as "municipal" or "emerging market." The program returns the results of the search as a hypertext list of fund names. Select any name and you will get several pages of information, including the following items:

The fund search utility is probably the best part of all of NETworth.

◆ Ticker symbol

◆ Total net assets

◆ Morningstar rating

◆ Objective

◆ Yield

◆ 3 Month / 1 Year / Year-to-Date average returns

◆ Fund description

◆ Minimum purchase and fee details

◆ Operational information

Morningstar provides this information on a quarterly basis for over 5,000 mutual funds.

As mentioned above, Level One provides NAV quotes, in chart and list format. Once again, you can search for a mutual fund either by ticker symbol or by string. You can select from several time periods for both the chart and list data. The chart can display the latest 10, 30, 90, or 300 days of unadjusted NAV prices; while the list can contain the latest 5, 20, 60, or 120 days of unadjusted NAV prices. The prices are updated daily from the NASDAQ via S&P Comstock. You have the ability to add or delete a selected fund to or from your portfolio.

Level One also presents information provided by the 100% No-Load Mutual Fund Council. This council is composed of true no-load mutual funds. Some readers may not know this, but funds with 12B-1 fees between zero and 0.25% are allowed to call themselves no-load funds (yes, a contradiction of terms, really). The Council has an excellent section titled the *Mutual Fund Investing Guide* which explains the basics of how mutual funds work, and what information is important to look for in a fund. This guide includes a *Glosssary of Mutual Fund Terms* that is very useful as well. Thirty-nine fund families are presented in this section, with over 200 specific funds profiled.

The remainder of Levels One, Two, and Three feature numerous mutual fund families with varying amounts of general and specific information. You can request that printed materials be sent to you from all fund sections. This is supposedly one of the advantages of using NETworth—that you can conveniently order a prospectus through the Internet and receive it as quickly if not more quickly than ordering one over the phone or by mail directly from the mutual fund family in question. I have found the opposite to be true, unfortunately. In several tests, it took about three to four weeks to receive a prospectus that I ordered through NETworth, whereas it took only one to two weeks to receive a prospectus that I ordered over the telephone from several mutual fund families.

NETworth lets you request that printed materials be sent to you from all fund sections.

NETworth lists in its Main Menu page another section, the *Internet Information Center*, that provides additional sources of information on topics related to mutual funds. In this area, you can get information about Morningstar's products, the Mutual Fund Education Alliance, and the 401(k) Association.

Wall Street Direct

http://www.cts.com:80/~wallst/

I discuss Wall Street Direct primarily in the Technical Analysis section later in Part Two. This site has several areas that directly pertain to the analysis of mutual funds. The *Products and Services* section of this Web page covers mutual funds in its bookstore and product-review areas. The bookstore lists books based on category. The mutual fund category is probably the weakest section of the bookstore, with only five books referenced. The last time I viewed the product-review area, it contained a detailed review of a popular mutual fund analysis program called Investor's FastTrack. Over time, you may see reviews on other mutual fund products as well.

The Specials and Demos section of the Web page has had demo versions of several mutual fund products—for example, Investor's FastTrack and Monocle—the last couple of times that I visited the area. You can download the demo(s) to your own computer and check out the product. They plan to add shareware programs for downloading in the future as well. This is a good area worth checking out periodically.

Futures and Options

This section has an interesting group of Internet sites. Some sites in this category just provide general information about the futures and options markets, while others provide pricing programs, and still others disseminate information pertaining to prices and events that might influence prices.

Chicago Mercantile Exchange

http://www.cme.com/cme/

This is an interesting page (see Figure 2.14). Although it doesn't provide much in the way of directly useful information for most individual investors, it does contain a wealth of historical (and impressive) information about the exchange, updates about new financial products and related services, and (perhaps most useful) a glossary of futures-related terms. All of the information is well written for the layperson. The glossary contains simplistic, but

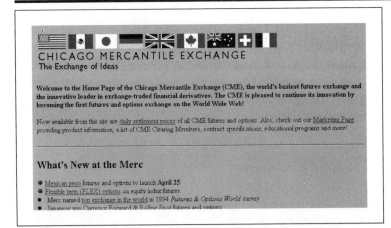

Figure 2.14: This site is interesting to browse, but provides only limited information about the futures and commodities markets.

clear, definitions. If you are interested in the world of futures and options, this is a good source to pick up background knowledge. The area mostly serves as a marketing tool. The site would be more useful to individual investors if it contained more information about futures and options, such as how they are used by various entities, what their risk characteristics are, how to price them, and so on.

Current Daily Oil and Gas Pricing

http://baervan.nmt.edu/prices/current.html

For those of you interested in the market prices of various forms of black gold (oil, that is), this site is for you. The Web page, shown in Figure 2.15, contains fairly detailed information about oil and several of its relatives. You can get price information about propane, natural gas, unleaded gas, West Texas Intermediate (WTI) Sweet, WTI Sour, and other specific types of crude.

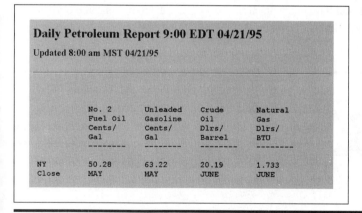

Daily Petroleum Report 9:00 EDT 04/21/95

Updated 8:00 am MST 04/21/95

	No. 2 Fuel Oil Cents/ Gal	Unleaded Gasoline Cents/ Gal	Crude Oil Dlrs/ Barrel	Natural Gas Dlrs/ BTU
	--------	--------	--------	--------
NY Close	50.28 MAY	63.22 MAY	20.19 JUNE	1.733 JUNE

Figure 2.15:
Want up-to-date prices on petroleum products? Look here.

Freese Notis Weather

http://www.weather.net/

Many commodities prices are directly affected by the behavior of weather. A bad freeze or excessive rains, for example, can result in poor crop yields which would decrease supply and increase prices. The Freese Notis company out of Des Moines, Iowa provides special weather forecasts to commodities investors. This Web page, shown in Figure 2.16, provides a rather nice summary of weather information. You can get the basic forecast for U.S. weather conditions. It also provides domestic and international weather conditions as they pertain to such commodities as Brazilian coffee, Argentine soy, South African corn, Northern European sugar beets, and Midwestern winter wheat. They have a Professional Traders Index that organizes information by the following commodity classes:

◆ Grain

◆ Food and Fiber

◆ Energy

◆ Livestock

This area is free; for a fee, however, they offer more timely and detailed reporting services. Unless you are in the commodities business, you probably do not have much practical use for this site. Freese-Notis also offers its services through QuoteCom's Web page for a fee.

Figure 2.16:
This Web will keep you up on the weather, but it's not for deciding what to wear to work.

Huang Weekly Futures Market Report

pcyhuang@tpts1.seed.net.tw

wuecon.wustl.edu

Paul Huang publishes a weekly report listing the performance of various futures securities since the previous report. You can send subscription requests to him via e-mail at pcyhuang@tpts1.seed.net.tw. Another location, the Washington University Economics Gopher, contains a historical directory of his reports. You can access that Gopher at wuecon.wustl.edu through port number 671. Refer to the Economics section later in Part Two for more information about this Gopher and its resources.

The weekly performance calculations are based on the future's return relative to its initial margin requirement. Futures covered include:

◆ Crude Oil, Gold, Silver, Platinum, Copper

◆ BPound, Can.$, DMark, Sw. Franc, Yen, Taiwan$, US$ Index

◆ Hang Seng, Nikkei, S&P 500, and Taiwan Stock Indexes

◆ US Treasury Bond, US Treasury Note, EuroDollar

◆ Cocoa, Coffee, Cotton, Sugar, Soy Beans/Meal/Oil, CRB Index

Huang also includes a series of news items pertaining to the futures markets. These items cover new products, regulations, and current events. For example, a recent report included several news items commenting about regulatory changes on the SIMEX exchange after the Barings/Leeson futures trading scandal.

Mantic Software Corp.

ftp.csn.org

This organization produces several option programs. These programs are basically educational in nature. The developers have done a good job developing the software in Windows and incorporating a thoughtful and interactive interface. The online help systems are excellent. They have a program, Options Laboratory, available for purchase at approximately $129, and a freeware program, Binomial Market Model.

Use Anonymous FTP to obtain a copy of the Binomial Market Model program. Connect to ftp.csn.org and go to the directory /mantic (see Figure 2.17) where you will find the following three files to retrieve:

binmrkt.zip

ftpinfo.txt

unzip.exe

Retrieve the files in binary mode and put them in an empty subdirectory on your computer. Read the ftpinfo.txt file to get instructions about installing the program. The Binomial Market Model program will teach you about the concept of volatility—what it is and how it is calculated. It is an educational tool, so use it as such. I downloaded, installed, and ran it with no problems. The program appears to be well designed and the documentation is certainly top notch.

Mantic reports that the freeware program was "distributed at this year's Financial Management Association annual meeting in St. Louis, and is being adopted by several universities in conjunction with courses on options or derivatives."

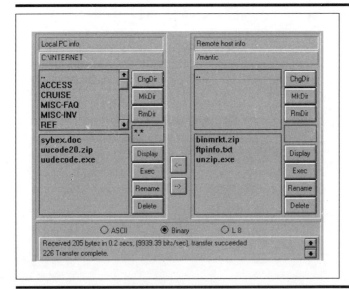

Figure 2.17:
Get free educational software on options from this FTP site.

The Mining Channel

http://www.wimsey.com:80/xr-cgi-bin/select?/6@/Magnet/mc/cover.html

This Web page provides rather scant data on obscure mining companies. I would approach the comments and recommendations made in this area with a good deal of skepticism. For example, of the seven companies listed when I first looked at this site, all were priced under $1 Canadian and five were listed on the Vancouver Stock Exchange (which has a reputation for less than stringent regulation). This area lacks any substantive background information relating to the issues about investing in mining companies. I only include a mention of this site here because you will likely see it listed as an Internet information resource at a number of other investment sites. Figure 2.18 shows you The Mining Channel under its new name, The Investor Channel.

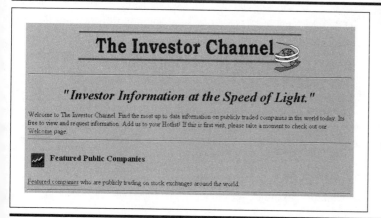

Figure 2.18:
This Web site has recently changed its name but has the same limited set of information.

misc.invest.futures

misc.invest.futures

This newsgroup belongs to the family of misc.invest newsgroups and addresses the subject of futures, along with related topics such as options. Compared to newsgroups in general, activity is below average: you normally see about 10 to 20 postings a day. The quality of discussion varies from poor to excellent.

Discussions cover such topics as specific aspects of a commodity, like cotton or silver; how to trade spreads, such as heating oil against crack oil; the differences between American and European style options, and why someone would want to exercise their option before expiration day; and individuals' comments and experiences with classes and training programs for trading commodities.

PitStar BBS Futures Page Quote

listserv@pitstar.com

wuecon.wustl.edu

This BBS provides daily end-of-day quotes for a number of futures contracts. You can get these quotes either by subscribing to their mailing list or by using Gopher to access an archive of their reports. To subscribe to the mailing list, you must send an e-mail message to listserv@pitstar.com and include the text sub quote-page *name@connection* in the body of the message where you replace *name@connection* with your e-mail address. By using Gopher, you can access the WU-Econ (Washington University Department of Economics) site, which contains historical archives of the daily PitStar report. This site is covered in the Economics section of Part Two.

The report lists open, high, low, close, last, volume, and open interest figures along with contract expiration date for a little over three dozen different futures securities, including:

◆ DMark, Australian$, Sw Franc, Yen, Bpound, Canad.$, US$

◆ Treasury Bonds/Notes/Bills, EuroDollar, Muni Bond

◆ Gold, Copper, Palladium, Platinum, Silver

◆ Heating Oil, Crude Oil, Unleaded Gas, Natural Gas

◆ Corn, Oat, Wheat, Soybeans, Soymeal, Soybean Oil

◆ Feeder Cattle, Live Cattle, Live Hogs, Pork Bellies

◆ Lumber, Cotton, Cocoa, Coffee, Sugar, Orange Juice

Robert's Online Option Pricer!

http://www.capmkt.com/services/option-pricer.html

This is a very simple page. It basically consists of two parts, the calculator and the background on options (see Figure 2.19). The calculator is basically a list of text boxes that prompt you to enter the primary inputs responsible for determining the theoretical value of an option. These include:

◆ Price of the Underlying Asset

◆ Strike Price

◆ Dividend Yield

◆ Interest Rate

◆ Volatility

◆ Time to Expiration

◆ Call or Put

◆ American or European Style

Robert's Online Option Pricer!

How much is the stock price? (in $.c)   `50.0000`

What is the strike price? (in $.c)   `55.0000`

What is the dividend yield? (in percentages per annum)   `3.00`

What is the interest rate? (in percentages per annum)   `9.00`

What is the volatility? (in percentages per annum)   `20.00`

How long left to expiration?   `9.0000`

Expiration in: ○ Days or ... ⦿ Months or ... ○ Years?

⦿ Call option or ... ○ Put option? ⦿ American option or ... ○ European option?
Now press   **Price it**

Figure 2.19:
Once here, you can calculate the price of an option.

After entering values for each of these inputs, you submit the entry and the calculator displays the theoretical value of the option along with some related pieces of information (delta, gamma, and theta). This option calculator is designed specifically to calculate the value of a stock option, and it has a number of general assumptions built into it. While useful in a general context, I would not use it as my sole source of information.

The second part provides background information about options and how they are priced. This part does only an average job of covering a large and complex body of knowledge. Given the nature of options, I think that this section should be more clear and concise in the wording of definitions and explanations.

Wall Street Direct

http://www.cts.com:80/~wallst/

I discuss Wall Street Direct primarily in the next section, Technical Analysis. The *Products and Services* section of this Web page has a bookstore area that lists books based on category. Categories here that are directly relevant to futures and options include Commodities, Currency, and Options. A large number of books are referenced in these three categories, and some books are listed in several categories.

Technical Analysis

This section deals with sites that have resources useful in carrying out technical analysis. Most of the sites either allow you to view price charts or download historical price data series that you can then use to create your own charts. Currently, you do not have the capability to perform sophisticated forms of technical analysis on the Internet. You cannot do trendline analysis, use technical indicators in a flexible manner, set up trading systems and backtest or optimize them, or perform technical screening. Telescan will help to alleviate this weakness as they make their online services available over the Internet. I expect that you will see this area grow rapidly in the near future. While it may seem like a lot is currently available, the current services are weak in the overall scope of technical analysis.

Experimental Stock Market Data

http://www.ai.mit.edu/stocks.html

This popular site is run by Mark Torrance at the AI Lab of MIT as an experiment. The site provides charts of close to 400 stocks (see the Web site in Figure 2.20).

If you can't find a stock, don't send e-mail to Mark Torrance—he doesn't control the list of securities, he just receives the data from a secondary source.

As far as I can tell, the prices date back to August 30, 1993 for all of the stocks listed. The charts are simple and basic—they show you price and volume along with performance relative to the S&P 500 index. The main limitation is that you cannot perform any further technical analysis at the site. You can, however, download the historical price data in ASCII format and use it with a technical analysis program on your own computer.

Experimental Stock Market Data

Prices have not been updated since April 14, 1995. The Stockmaster is aware of the problem and is working on it. Mutual Fund prices are current to April 21, 1995.

This is an experimental page that currently provides a link to the latest stock market information. It is updated automatically, usually between 10:00 p.m. EDT and 1:00 a.m. EDT, from an email source in California to reflect the current day's closing information. It consists of general market news and quotes for selected stocks. Not all stocks are included here, see here for the ticker symbols of the included stocks.

Stock prices are "Deemed reliable, but never guaranteed." For reliable stock prices consult a licensed stockbroker or a reputable financial newspaper or service. For more information about the source of these quotes, or to get on the mailing list to receive these quotes directly please contact *martin.wong@eng.sun.com*. The charts available below are part of a free

Figure 2.20: Want to get free price charts on hundreds of popular stocks? If so, this is the place to look.

You can also get charts of some mutual funds. The charts simply display a graph of the fund's price over time. The various mutual funds included have different starting dates. The same limitations of the stock charts apply to these charts of mutual funds.

The mutual funds are not automatically updated; nor are they adjusted for distributions—so do not use their charts here as a basis for making any related investment decisions!

This Web page also provides some other information as well. One section lists the most frequently requested stocks. It is not all too surprising that this list tends to be dominated by computer and communications technology stocks. Another section provides data for the latest trading day, and includes

◆ Closing Price

◆ Total Change from the Previous Close

◆ Percentage Change from the Previous Close

◆ High Price

◆ Low Price

◆ Previous Closing Price

◆ Volume in Number of Shares Traded

◆ Volume in Dollar Value of Shares Traded

You can also view a list of all stocks included, sorted in alphabetical order by either name or ticker symbol. Several other sections let you download the latest daily update or historical data files. You can also download this information by using anonymous FTP to connect to ftp.ai.mit.edu. Then go to the directory /pub/stocks/results/ to select one or more files to retrieve.

HedgeHog

http://risc.cpbx.net/hedgehog/WelToHH.html

This site functions like an online newsletter (see Figure 2.21). You can subscribe to receive HedgeHog newsletters, electronically, for $225 per annum or $60 per quarter (the first month is available as a free trial copy). It is published the second week of each month, and is updated as market conditions change. You receive technical analyses and commentaries on several markets including:

◆ Dow Indexes

◆ S&P 500

◆ S&P 100

◆ NYSE

◆ Gold

◆ CRB Index

◆ Six Major Currencies

The newsletter has charts for the various markets that are covered. The charts include a number of technical indicators in multiple colors. The newsletter also has editorial articles.

HedgeHog provides a tutorial database that discusses the application of technical analysis, particularly the use of various oscillators to detect changes in trend. It also has a glossary of technical analysis and option-related terms.

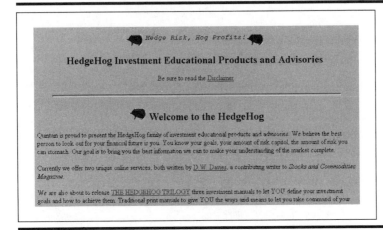

Intelligent Market Analytics, Inc.

http://www.marketmind.com/

This site, shown in Figure 2.22, is basically just an advertisement for the product that Intelligent Market Analytics, Inc. sells, which is called *MarketMind*. This program requires that you have either SuperCharts or TradeStation, both of which are technical analysis programs sold by Omega Research. MarketMind sounds like it is a weighted pattern-recognition type of trading system. It carries a fairly hefty price tag as well—$269 to get SuperCharts, MarketMind, and some data. After 30 days, you must pay $650

if you wish to become a registered user of MarketMind. You can download a demo and the documentation for MarketMind. Although I am familiar with SuperCharts and can say that it is a good technical analysis program, I am not familiar with MarketMind. That does not mean the program is bad, it just means that I can't give you any comments about its strengths and weaknesses.

misc.invest.technical

misc.invest.technical

Yet another member of the misc.invest family of newsgroups. This one has moderate activity with approximately 20 to 30 postings per day. It covers topics that pertain to technical analysis. Most of the postings concern some aspect of using a computer to perform technical analysis. The popular charting programs—MetaStock, SuperCharts, and Windows on WallStreet, are discussed frequently here. You also see timing programs, such as OmniTrader by Nirvana, bandied about in this newsgroup. Postings discuss the basic features of these programs, how to use certain features, how to set up custom indicators, and satisfaction/dissatisfaction with technical support and documentation.

Readers also discuss general topics relating to technical analysis, such as the merits of market timing in general, how to use Candlestick charting, and sources of historical data. This area has a relatively low amount of garbage postings and is definitely worth checking out if you are considering getting into technical analysis or already use it.

Ohio State University Finance Department

http://www.cob.ohio-state.edu/dept/fin/osudata.html

This site has very limited resources, but is sort of interesting to check out. It contains some historical data on interest rates, Treasury Bond futures price ticks, and the Dow Jones Industrial Average. You can get weekly and daily data on the Dow Jones Industrial Average for the periods 1900 to 1989 and 1915 to 1989, respectively. It includes high, low, close, and volume figures. I mention this site primarily because this information is difficult to get ahold of at a reasonable price.

Free historical price data should be examined carefully for integrity. Managing this type of information is a labor-intensive task, so it is wise to be suspect of data integrity, even for data sold commercially.

One reason this site is interesting is that it has historical data for France and England back in the 1700s. I have not examined this information, but for those with an active curiosity this should make for some fun adventure.

QuoteCom

ftp.quote.com

http://www.quote.com/

In this entry I focus on the parts of QuoteCom that can be used for technical analysis. (I cover most of QuoteCom's services in the section on Fundamental Stock Analysis earlier in Part Two; I also cover some of its features under the Portfolio Management section.)

You can get end-of-day price updates for securities listed on domestic exchanges as a part of QuoteCom's *Basic Service*, which costs $9.95 per month. The end-of-day update files are available via QuoteCom's FTP server, ftp.quote.com, in the directory /pub/updates. There are two subdirectories here that contain useful information:

/current

/statistics

Other directories exist, but you need to subscribe to the related service to access files with one of those directories (or pay a high marginal fee per file downloaded). Within each of these subdirectories you will find numerous sets of files.

The best way to learn what each file contains is to get any and all messages, "readme," and instruction types of files provided in each subdirectory. When you use FTP to get update files, you will need to use FTP; anonymous FTP will not work. Enter your login name and password when connecting to QuoteCom's server.

The /pub/updates/current subdirectory contains many files, each one summarizing price information for a particular exchange. Each file appears in both full and compressed sizes. Files are named for the exchange and date. For example, the file containing price updates for NYSE stocks on February 24 of the current year is titled nyse0224.txt. The data inside the file is comma-delimited. Each line has the ticker symbol, date, and price.

The /pub/updates/statistics subdirectory contains files that provide summary information about a particular exchange. For example, the file acq0224.txt provides a listing of the most active stocks on the NASDAQ exchange for February 24 of the current year. This directory also has graphic charts of four market indexes: the Dow Jones Industrials, S&P 500, S&P 100, and NASDAQ Composite. These files are actually updated periodically intraday while the markets are open.

QuoteCom offers a *Chart Service* at a rate of $9.95 per month (you are limited to a maximum of 50 charts per day). Nonsubscribers can use the service for 39 cents per chart. This service is fairly plain, but it is a step above the features offered in MIT's Experimental Stock Market Data site. You must use a Web browser to access this service. You can get charts on all domestic securities covered in Basic services and on securities listed on

You can get charts on all domestic securities covered in QuoteCom's Basic services and on securities listed on any foreign exchanges that you subscribe to.

any foreign exchanges that you subscribe to. The charts are only updated after the end of each trading day, usually around 5:15pm EST.

You have the ability to control a chart's timespan, time periods (daily, weekly, monthly), type (bar, candlestick, or closing price), color scheme, volume or open interest, and moving average parameters (none, simple, weighted, exponential, time period). You use simple pop-up boxes to select a chart's features. In the future, QuoteCom will be adding more technical indicators.

The graphs are not really that impressive in presentation. If you have ever used a technical analysis program like MetaStock, SuperCharts, or Windows on WallStreet, the QuoteCom charts will seem rather plain. This area is probably most useful to the individual who just wants to look at price charts occasionally to get a graphic indication of how a security is performing. This service does not currently provide a useful level of features to those who want to perform intermediate to advanced levels of technical analysis.

QuoteCom also provides historical price data. The cost is $1.95 per file. By using FTP, you can view the size of a file before downloading, to gauge the amount of historical data (larger files will contain more history). Use FTP to connect to ftp.quote.com (logging in with your username and password), and go to the directory /pub/history/ which has 31 subdirectories itself. Each of these 31 subdirectories is for a particular exchange (such as NYSE) or subject (such as indexes). The foreign indexes do not currently have historical data, but should soon (Canadian data is already available). The index subdirectory is very detailed, including indexes from a number of foreign countries. Files are in ASCII comma-delimited format. The following histories are available:

Stocks	Starting 1988
Mutual Funds	Starting 1992
Commodities	Starting April 1992

Savage Archives

dg-rtp.dg.com

The Savage Archives are a hodgepodge collection of various forms of historical data. Use anonymous FTP to connect to the site listed at the beginning of this entry and go to the subdirectory /pub/misc.invest/ to see a couple of files and a listing of about one dozen subdirectories. While there are a few interesting files, such as one that has monthly figures from 1965 to mid-1994 on a half dozen economic indicators, the data is uploaded from a variety of individuals and the time periods are sporadic.

Also, many files are named using Unix conventions, with long names and/or multiple periods. These types of file names are incompatible with DOS-based operating systems, so your only alternative is to use FTP in a Unix command-line interface, get the files, rename them to a DOS-compatible format, and then download them to your computer. This does not make for a productive use of one's time.

If you need historical price data, you will probably be better off finding a site or service that gets the data from one source. You'll do even better if the place manages the data themselves. While this will usually cost money, it can be worth it to have a high degree of confidence in the accuracy of the data.

Telescan

http://www.telescan.com/

You may have heard of Telescan outside of the Internet world. Telescan is primarily known as an online service that focuses on providing financial information and software (see Figure 2.23). It has been around for a number of years and markets online and offline products that include:

◆ Charting Software

◆ Screening Software

◆ Option Analysis

◆ News Services

Telescan announced in February of 1995 that it will be providing Internet users with "complete access" to their software, databases, and information resources. The Web page is currently up, but is under construction. Time will tell how this area turns out; Telescan has announced that you will be able to get real-time updates (this may not include quotes).

You will most likely have to pay for these services. The way the current online service works (which you cannot access via the Internet), you can sign up for basic service, which includes the Analyzer (a chart retrieval and technical analysis program that retrieves and charts historical price data on a wide range of securities, including stocks, indexes, mutual funds, futures,

Welcome to the Telescan World Wide Web Server!

Telescan Inc. is a worldwide leader in the development of interactive online information systems among businesses, individuals, government agencies, and non-profit organizations through the delivery of superior, cost effective data retrieval technology, custom user interface programs and online communications services. This World Wide Web server is a continuation of our commitment to provide superior customer support and information about our products and services.

Telescan hopes you find our WWW server a convenient and effective way to request literature, download software applications, review product information, and receive valuable services directly through your Web browser.

Figure 2.23: This site will offer an increasingly wide array of services. If you want powerful charting on the Internet, look here.

and options). You also get access to a number of news services, some of which are free (Comtex and Reuters newswires), along with others that charge per report (S&P MarketScope, SEC Online, and Zacks Investment Service).

Other programs offered by Telescan (which cost extra) provide you with the ability to filter stocks, mutual funds, and options, based on different sets of conditions. By the time this book comes out in print Telescan should have announced more details about what will specifically be offered through the Internet.

One area, Investor Resources, has an Encyclopedia of Indicators that provides definitions and explanations for a rather comprehensive list of technical (and some fundamental) indicators.

Wall Street Direct

http://www.cts.com:80/~wallst/

I must say that this was one of the first sites to really impress me. Wall Street Direct has done an excellent job setting up its Web page. Although the focus is clearly on market timing in general, and technical analysis in specific, this site does contain information on a number of other investment subjects. Refer to the appropriate sections in Part Two for further information regarding those aspects of this Web page (shown in Figure 2.24).

The first part of Wall Street Direct's home page is the *Products and Services* area. It offers a number of resources, including:

◆ Book Review

◆ Bookstore

◆ Press Releases

◆ Software Reviews

◆ Trader's Glossary

The *Book Review* area features a detailed review of one book. The review provides a good amount of information. I would like to see an archive of past reviews, and reviews of previously released books for that matter. Such additions would be particularly useful in this field, where books tend to have a lengthy lifespan.

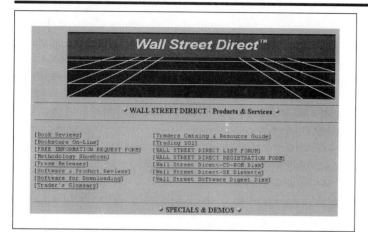

Wall Street Direct™

↝ WALL STREET DIRECT · Products & Services ↝

[Book Reviews]   [Traders Catalog & Resource Guide]
[Bookstore On-Line]   [Trading 101]
[FREE INFORMATION REQUEST FORM]   [WALL STREET DIRECT LIST FORUM]
[Methodology ShowDown]   [WALL STREET DIRECT REGISTRATION FORM]
[Press Releases]   [Wall Street Direct-CD-ROM Disk]
[Software & Product Reviews]   [Wall Street Direct-SE Diskette]
[Software for Downloading]   [Wall Street Software Digest Disk]
[Trader's Glossary]

↝ SPECIALS & DEMOS ↝

Figure 2.24:
Wall Street Direct
is an excellent
resource for the
technical analyst in
particular as well as
the general investor.

The *Online Bookstore* is very impressive. If I were going to set up a comprehensive library of investment books from scratch, the inventory of this area would take care of almost all of my needs. The bookstore organizes materials into 13 categories (like Bonds, Currency, Cycles, Market Psychology, Market Timing, System Design, etc.), with many books appearing in several categories. Upon selecting a specific title, you see the author, description, and price.

The *Press Releases* area contains a wide variety of interesting and pertinent news items. Items tend to be several paragraphs in length and cover such topics as new investment software programs and upgrades to existing ones, pension portfolios looking into the use of commodities, and the CBOE's implementing wireless, hand-held market-maker terminals.

Software Reviews lists several dozen products that have been reviewed. The last time that I examined this area, 10 out of the 34 reviews could be viewed. You must order a diskette to get the full set of reviews. The reviews were lengthy, detailed, and well written. The majority of the products covered here are technically oriented.

The *Trader's Glossary* provides definitions to several dozen technical and fundamental terms. The definitions are fairly well detailed. I think that this area could be easily improved by expanding the breadth and depth of terms, especially considering the detail that WSD has in its other areas. A number of other areas are listed in this first section of WSD's Web page, including order and subscription information. This is a good area to check out, regardless of what type of investor you might be.

Specials and Demos is the second major section of WSD's Web page. It includes a number of demo (demonstration) versions of popular software programs like MetaStock and Investor's FastTrack. It will also be adding shareware programs in the near future. This section also contains some advertisements about various events and products. For example, when I last connected there was an item about a risk management conference and a listing about Stock Data Corp., a vendor of historical price data.

The last major section to WSD's Web page is its *Yellow Pages Listings*. This section contains directory listings of such resources as

◆ Broker services

◆ Catalogs

◆ Educational organizations and products

◆ Magazines and newspapers

◆ Newsletter services

◆ Software demo listings

◆ Audio/video services

Wall Street Software

http://www-bprc.mps.ohio-state.edu/cgi-bin/hpp?wsshome.html

This Web page is pretty basic and brief. It consists of three parts: cross-links to other investment sites, programs that you can download, and an order/ registration area.

The software download section has fewer than 10 programs to choose from and all but two are demo (demonstration) programs. Each program is given a brief description, and the size of the file is listed. When I last accessed the site, the download area had one shareware program, Chart-Util, and demos of two popular technical analysis programs—MetaStock Pro 4.5 and MegaTech.

This site might develop into a much more useful resource once it adds content: more demos and shareware and freeware, for example.

Windows on WallStreet

mktarts@netcom.com

If you use MarketArts' technical analysis program, Windows on WallStreet (WOW), you can get customer service by sending an e-mail message to the above address. They also have a mailing list that you can join by sending a message to listserv@netcom.com (include the text subscribe wowtalk-l) in the body of the message. They will supposedly be adding FTP and Web sites shortly.

These existing and future areas will be useful to WOW users and might also be of value to individuals with a general interest in technical analysis. WOW is currently one of the three most popular technical analysis programs available for IBM-compatible PC's running Windows. It is geared primarily for the beginner to intermediate technical analyst and costs approximately $150 for the retail version and $250 for the professional version. Don't let the titles fool you—even beginners can benefit greatly from using the professional version, it is not designed solely for the trading gurus.

The other two leading technical analysis programs for IBM-compatible PC's are MetaStock, by Equis, and SuperCharts, by Omega Research. MetaStock is available in DOS and Windows versions and provides capabilities for advanced users, but is easy for beginners to use and costs around $350. SuperCharts runs under Windows only, is easy to use, provides more capabilities than WOW but less than MetaStock, and costs around $250.

Economic Analysis

This topic could be the focus of an entire book, as it is really a sibling field to that of finance/investing. I have focused the discussion in this section to cover the sites that apply most directly to individual investors, primarily sites that provide data about economic figures that the market views as important. For those of you interested in getting more information about economic theory or forecasting, I would suggest that you look at the sites run by a university Economics Department; they provide many links to this type of information if they don't in fact have it themselves.

FRED—Federal Reserve Economic Data

(314) 621-1824

FRED is a bulletin board service operated by the Federal Reserve Bank of St. Louis. It is not accessible through the Internet yet; however, an individual I spoke to there responded that it was being considered. I think that there is a good chance that FRED will become accessible via the Internet, but if it doesn't, I recommend that you still check it out by dialing the number above with your modem; the place has a wealth of economic and financial data available for downloading.

The financial data available is covered in the Fixed-Income Analysis section earlier in Part Two. This includes such data as historical interest rate series for Federal Funds and for Discount, Prime, Corporate, and Treasury securities. In this entry I'll cover the economic data available.

FRED has files organized into 28 separate directories. See the list that accompanies the FRED entry under the Fixed Income Analysis section for a complete listing of the directories. The second directory, *Historical Data—Monetary Aggregates*, includes files containing monthly M1, M2, and M3 money stock (money supply) numbers dating from 1959 to present. The

Business/Fiscal Data directory includes figures for economic data, like capacity utilization (dating from 1965 to present), and federal debt (dating from 1955 to present). The *Consumer Price Index* (CPI) and *Producer Price Index* (PPI) directories contain many different cross-sections of CPI and PPI figures, respectively, some starting as early as 1913. The *International Data* directory has files containing similar data for the other major industrialized countries, including Canada, France, Germany, Italy, Japan, and the United Kingdom. It also has exchange rates for a number of countries' currencies versus the U.S. dollar, all starting in 1980 and running up to the present.

All in all, FRED is an excellent source of well-organized historical data. Many people would benefit greatly by FRED becoming available via the Internet. As you will see later in this section, another government entity, the Department of Commerce, has already made several of its databases (STAT-USA) available through the Internet.

Modern Portfolio Management

http://www.magibox.net/~mpm

I discuss this Web page primarily in the Portfolio Management section earlier in Part Two; however, it provides some resources for other areas of investing, including economic analysis.

The MPM Web page has a *Research Center* that provides several lists containing information about popular economic indicators. Interest rates are listed separately. The interest rate list describes the current yield of several fixed-income security classes over multiple maturity horizons. The economic indicator list includes such information as:

◆ Report Date and Time

◆ Paine Webber's Estimates

◆ Consensus Estimates

◆ Actual Values

You can also view the four latest lists for economic indicators (only the most recent interest rate history list is available). From the home page, select *Free Subscription Services*. Select the hypertext link named *View a Brief History of Important Economic Indicators*.

You can subscribe to receive free weekly updates for the economic indicator list. Simply send an e-mail message to mlong@baste.magibox.net and include the text subscribe WEI in the body of the message. Expect to receive an average of four updates per week.

STAT-USA

 ftp.stat-usa.gov

 ebb.stat-usa.gov

 Gopher.stat-usa.gov

 http://www.stat-usa.gov/

STAT-USA is a part of the Economics and Statistics Administration which is in turn a part of the U.S. Department of Commerce. STAT-USA provides Internet access to three different databases of information:

◆ National Trade Data Bank (NTDB)

◆ National Economic, Social, and Environmental Data Bank (NESE)

◆ Economic Bulletin Board (EBB)

Of these three databases, the Economic Bulletin Board offers the most useful information to individual investors. The NTDB focuses on exports and imports, and the NESE on social programs; the EBB covers the economic statistics that are most frequently used in analyzing the financial markets. The EBB divides the information it supplies into 30 subjects:

AgWorld International Ag Situation Reports

Best Market Reports

Current Business Statistics

Defense Conversion Subcommittee Information

Eastern Europe Trade Leads

Economic Indicators

Employment Statistics

Energy Statistics

Foreign Assets Control Program

Foreign Trade

General Information Files

Industrial Sector Analysis Reports

Industry Statistics

International Market Insight Reports

Miscellaneous Economic Files

Miscellaneous Files

Miscellaneous Trade Files

Monetary Statistics

National Export Strategy Files

National Income and Products Accounts

Press Releases from the U.S. Trade Representative

Price and Productivity Statistics

Regional Economic Statistics

Software International Articles

Special Studies and Reports

State-by-State Export Resource Listings

Summaries of Current Economic Conditions

Trade Opportunity Program

U.S. Department of Agriculture Leads

U.S. Treasury Auction Results

Most of the subjects are probably too focused to be of interest; however, the Economic Indicators, Monetary Statistics, Price and Productivity Statistics, and the U.S. Treasury Auction Results will have wide appeal and useful information.

You can access STAT-USA in a variety of ways—FTP, Telnet (EBB only), Gopher, and World Wide Web (see Figure 2.25 for the Web page). FTP and Gopher access to the NTDB and NESE data banks is free; Web access is not. If you wish to use a Web browser, the cost is $8.35 per month for unlimited access. For convenience, you can subscribe for one year at a flat $100 (a whopping savings of twenty cents!). Unfortunately, the most useful of the three data banks costs the most. EBB has an annual subscription fee of $45, which includes a credit of $20 to be applied to connect-time charges (yes, this means more fees follow—in addition to the annual subscription, EBB charges you for the length of time that you stay connected to their system). Per-minute connect charges vary depending on time of access, as follows:

Time	Billing Rate
8am to Noon EST, M–F	$0.40/minute
Noon to 6pm EST, M–F	$0.30/minute
6pm to 8am EST, M–F (and all day on weekends and federal holidays)	$0.10/minute

On the Internet, you can only access the EBB via Telnet at ebb.stat-usa.gov (it also operates as a Bulletin Board, but most users would incur expensive long-distance charges). If you do not have a subscription and want to see specific examples of what they offer, log in under the username guest and you will be provided with limited access.

Figure 2.25: Get economic data straight from the horse's mouth.

STAT·USA

A division of the Economics and Statistics Administration of the U.S. Department of Commerce.

STAT-USA is THE Internet source for business and economic information produced by the Federal Government. STAT-USA gathers the most crucial, timely business and economic information from over 50 Federal agencies and distributes from a central source: true low-cost, one-stop shopping, saving you countless hours in research time.

Contents

- About STAT-USA and How to Register
- STAT-USA On-Line Information Services----NTDB--NESE--BEA

Although you must pay to get direct access to the EBB's resources, you can get this information indirectly at no cost through several university Gopher sites. The University of Michigan downloads data from EBB. Although the downloads appear to be complete and timely, UMich cannot guarantee this. Washington University of St. Louis has a cross-link in their WU-Econ site to UMich's Gopher. If you are a casual user these free sites are probably the best bet, but if you depend on timely and complete updates you should consider getting the data straight from its source—the EBB.

University of Michigan—EBB Data

una.hh.lib.umich.edu

You can connect to this Gopher at the above site. Make sure to set the port to 70 and the selector to 1/ebb if you are using a graphic Gopher interface. You will get a menu that displays the full set of Economic Bulletin Board (EBB) data that is available.

EBB is produced by STAT-USA, which is discussed in the previous entry. If you were to get EBB data directly from STAT-USA, you would have to pay subscription and connect-time charges; the University of Michigan downloads this information and makes it available to the public at no charge. The trade-off is that UMich cannot guarantee that its downloads are complete and timely.

The UMich site is cross-linked to the WU-Econ site, the topic of the next entry.

Washington University of St. Louis Economics Dept.

wuecon.wustl.edu

The Department of Economics at Washington University maintains a Gopher (WU-Econ) that provides access to economic and financial resources. Most of these resources are the product of individuals or organizations with no connection to the department.

One of the resources that offers access to academic research is the Economics Working Paper Archive. Papers are categorized by topic, such as:

◆ Econometrics

◆ Microeconomics

◆ Game Theory and Information

- Macroeconomics

- International Trade

- International Finance

- Finance

- Risk and Insurance

    Subtopics within these categories range from obscure to popular. For example, within the finance category I found one paper that dealt with "Stochastic Dominance, Pareto Optimality, and Equilibrium Asset Pricing," which did not sound like it had the potential for direct application to investing by individuals, whereas another paper dealt with a method for developing neural network based techniques that lead to "more robust forecasting along with a large amount of statistical information on forecast performance." It is safe to say that the majority of these papers use advanced mathematical techniques and would primarily be of use to the advanced investor.

    You will be likely to experience two problems finding papers of interest. First, the listings within each category are not intuitive (I think they were designed for use by economics students working on University Unix machines). Second, most of the papers are either in a compressed Unix format, or PostScript or Acrobat format. None of these can simply be downloaded and opened in a normal word processing program, which is what I, and probably most of you, normally do.

You can also find archives of popular reports such as Holts Reports, Huang's Weekly Futures Market, and the PitStar BBS Futures Page Quote in this Gopher.

    The WU-Econ Gopher has a cross-link to the University of Michigan Gopher, where EBB data, downloaded from STAT-USA, is available at no cost. (Both the STAT-USA and UMich sites are mentioned earlier in this section.) You can also find archives of popular reports such as Holts Reports, Huang's Weekly Futures Market, and the PitStar BBS Futures Page Quote in this Gopher. The Holts Reports are covered in the next section of Part Two—News, Quotes, and Market Statistics. I cover the other two resources in the Futures and Options section earlier in Part Two.

News, Quotes, and Market Statistics

These sites all act as conduits for you to get access to current events. This includes information about how the markets are performing, what the government is doing, and what companies are doing. This information is of different levels of importance to individuals, primarily in terms of its timeliness, but also in terms of scope and depth. The better the information, the more likely it is that you will have to pay to get it.

DowVision

http://dowvision.wais.net/

DowVision is run by Dow Jones and WAIS, Inc., and is published by Dow Jones Business Information Services. It is currently being beta-tested and is available to the public free of charge. DowVision will eventually become a commercial service. The service includes the full text of:

◆ The Wall Street Journal

◆ Dow Jones News Service

◆ Dow Jones International News Services

◆ Japan Economic Newswire

◆ Canada Newswire

◆ BusinessWire

◆ PR Newswire

◆ Investext Abstracts

◆ Professional Investor Report

DowVision has one feature—a search engine for finding news items (see Figure 2.26). This may not sound like much, but it is. You can get a massive amount of information by simply entering one or more words. The service then searches through all of the news articles and presents you with a list that includes the item(s) you specified.

There are a number of ways to search for news items, but not all of them are fully developed yet. First, you can restrict the scope of the search to a specific news source or leave it open to all sources. Second, you can choose to limit the number of matching items found to 3, 10, 40, 80, 120, 160, 200, 240, or 500. Third, in terms of subject matter, you can currently search by name. In the future you will also be able to search by source and by subject.

An example will highlight the strengths and weaknesses of what is currently available. Let's say that I wanted to search for news relating to a publicly listed stock on a company called Borden Chemicals and Plastics L.P. I could look for it by entering borden chemical, but I would also get articles on Borden and Chemical Bank because the search engine looks for matches against each individual word. The best way to get information on a specific stock is by entering its ticker symbol (of course you have to know the ticker first). I will then get a response listing the number of articles that I specified. I can select any individual story and will get the full text of that story. At the end of each article, cross-links appear for other categories such as industry, subject, market, and geographic location.

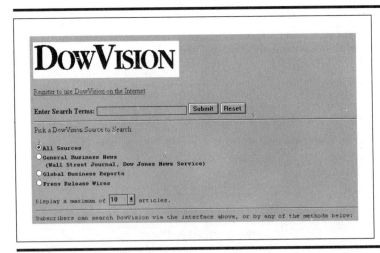

Figure 2.26: This site is under development, but does and will offer access to an impressive array of information.

In the future, you will be able to search by subject or source. Subject matter is already organized under seven different codes:

◆ Industry Group

◆ Market Sector

◆ News Subject

◆ Statistical

◆ Government

◆ Product

◆ Geographic

Industry group codes consist of approximately 120 categories which group over 20,000 public and private companies in the U.S. and abroad. These industry codes are linked to the market sector codes. Market sectors are divided into nine groups:

◆ Basic Materials

◆ Conglomerates

◆ Consumer (cyclical)

◆ Consumer (noncyclical)

◆ Energy

◆ Financial

◆ Industrial

◆ Technology

◆ Utilities

News subjects are divided into over 170 codes which fall into three general categories:

◆ Business, Financial, and General

◆ SEC Documents (federal filings only)

◆ Newswires

Statistical codes are separated into two broad categories—Financial Market Statistics and Economic Statistics. Government codes are grouped into over fifty categories, broadly falling under the Canada, Japan, U.K., and the U.S. There are over 25 Product codes. Geographic codes are split into four groups—Canada, U.S., Countries, and Regions. There are over 100 countries and 15 regions.

In addition to searching by subject, in the future you will also be able to search by news source. News sources consist of four broad categories:

◆ The Wall Street Journal

◆ Dow Jones News Services

◆ Dow Jones International News Services

◆ Press Wires

The current day's Wall Street Journal is available by 2:00am. Dow Jones News Services are updated continuously in real-time from 7:30am to 7:00pm each business day. Dow Jones International News Services are updated continuously from 6:00am on Sunday to 11:00am on Saturday, and this includes the European and Asian Wall Street Journals. The press wires are updated continuously, on a 15-minute delay, from 7:00am to 7:00pm each business day. All times are Eastern Standard Time.

DowVision is still under development. It is currently a great source of free information, but you may have to work a little at getting what you want (it's not that difficult though). In the future, however, you will have to weigh two factors that will change its value: the cost, and the functionality of the service. I recommend that you at least check it out while the service is still free. It has a wealth of good information.

Gruntal & Company—Weekly Market Summary

http://www.gruntal.com/investments/wms.html

Gruntal and Company make this site available for users with Web access. This is a simple, but useful, resource. The Web site's organization is clear and concise. You get a snapshot of several markets' behavior over a two-week timespan. Gruntal's home page (Figure 2.27) categorizes summary information in seven groups:

◆ Top and Bottom 10 Performers

◆ Dow Jones and Other Averages

◆ Money Rates

◆ New Highs and Lows

◆ Upcoming Earnings Announcements

◆ Gold and Silver

◆ Economic Pulse

The *Top 10/Bottom 10 Performers* lists the ten best and ten worst industry groups based on their percent change in price since the previous week's close. *Dow Jones and Other Averages* lists the close, change, percent change, average PE ratio, and average dividend yield for the Dow Jones (DJ) Industrial and DJ Transportation and DJ Utilities, the NASDAQ Composite, the S&P 500, and the Russell 1000 indexes. *Money Rates* lists, for the most recent week and previous week, the Discount, Prime, Federal Funds, Broker Call, 6-Month CD, and 2/5/10/30-Year Treasury Note and Bond interest rates.

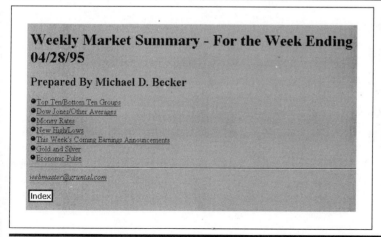

Figure 2.27: Here's a place to get summary market information, free.

New Highs and Lows lists the number of stocks that reached new high prices and those that hit new low prices for each of the NYSE, AMEX, and NASDAQ exchanges. *Upcoming Earnings Announcements* lists those stocks that are due to report quarterly earnings in the upcoming week and, for comparison, provides the company's earnings for the same quarter of the previous year. *Gold and Silver* lists the prices of gold and silver at the end of the most recent week and the previous week. *Economic Pulse* lists the inflation and unemployment rates for the most recent week and the previous week.

Although this site provides a weekly summary, I have known it to be off by one week at times. For example, on Sunday, March 12, I connected to this Web's home page and the information was for the week ending Friday, March 3. As a free source of information, one can hardly complain; however, be sure to check the date of information so that you know what it is you are looking at.

Holt's Reports

geoholt@netcom.com

misc.invest

ftp.netcom.com

wuecon.wustl.edu

http://turnpike.net/metro/holt/index.html

George Holt creates a regular set of four reports for each trading day. He makes these reports available to the public, free of charge, but does encourage people to send him donations if they value and use the reports. This runs along the same vein as the concept behind shareware programs. Each report contains summary information on a general subject. I find his reports to be useful and convenient and I recommend that you take a look at them. The four reports he produces are:

◆ Holt's Market Report

◆ Holt's Actives Report

◆ Holt's Volume Report

◆ Holt's Optionable Stock Report

You have several means of accessing the Holt reports. You can use anonymous FTP to access the FTP site listed at the beginning of this entry. Select ftp.netcom.com and go to the /pub/ge/geoholt subdirectory where you will find a file named holt_rpt.txt. This file contains all four reports for the latest completed trading day.

You can use Gopher to access the site wuecon.wustl.edu, which contains archives of past trading days' reports as well as the most recently completed trading day's report. Make sure that you use the port number 671 when connecting to this Gopher. You will see a directory titled Holt's Stock Market Reports. Select this directory and you will get a listing of the recent daily report files along with subdirectories for the months, starting back with February 1994. Each monthly subdirectory contains daily files for that period of time. As of March 1995, George Holt provides Web access to his reports. Figure 2.28 shows the Holt Report home page. The Web currently provides the most recent set of reports, but also has a hypertext cross-link to the WU-Econ gopher.

Holt's Market Report The Market Report has summary information on indexes, exchanges, currencies, gold, and interest rates. It is divided into five sections. The first section contains open, high, low, close, and total change from the previous day on 29 different domestic indexes. The second section has the same data on 10 foreign indexes. The third section provides breadth indicators for the NYSE, AMEX, and NASDAQ exchanges. The fourth section has exchange rates between the U.S. dollar and 18 foreign currencies, expressed both in terms of dollars per foreign currency and vice versa. The fifth section has the last, total change, and previous value for the price of gold and silver, and the current rates of Federal Funds, Prime, 3-month and 6-month Treasury Bills, 1/3/5/10-year Treasury Notes, and 30-year Treasury Bonds.

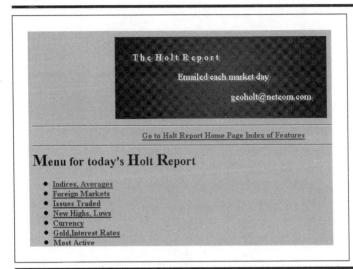

Figure 2.28:
The Holt Reports provide excellent summary information on a variety of domestic and international markets.

Holt's Actives Report The Actives Report lists the ten most active stocks for each of the NYSE, AMEX, and NASDAQ exchanges. Information presented includes company name, number of shares traded, closing price, and the change from the previous day's price.

Holt's Volume Report The Volume Report differs from the Actives Report in that it lists companies whose volume has increased by more than 50 percent. One list includes all of the companies from the NYSE, AMEX, and NASDAQ exchanges that satisfy the above condition. Another lists stocks that have reached new highs. The Volume Report also has these two lists for a special group of high-EPS growth stocks, so you end up with four lists altogether. Each list contains the following information for each stock: company name, ticker symbol, high, low, close, total volume, percent change in volume, total price change, and percent change in price.

Holt's Optionable Stock Report This report is very similar to the previous one in that it lists those stocks whose volume has increased by more than 50 percent and those stocks that have reached new highs. It also lists those stocks that have reached new lows. The difference is that the list is drawn from a database of all domestic stocks that have listed options trading on them. This database currently consists of 1,430 stocks. The same information about price and volume statistics in the Volume Report (the topic of the previous paragraph) is presented on each stock in this report.

InterQuote

info@paragon.wwa.com

iq.wwa.com

http://wwa.com/~quote/

Paragon Software brings you access to real-time, delayed, and closing end-of-day quotes (see Figure 2.29). The real-time service is not free; however, the delayed and closing quotes are both currently free. You can get price information on stocks, options, and indexes listed on the NYSE, AMEX, NAS-DAQ, Chicago Mercantile Exchange (CME), and Option Price Reporting Authority (OPRA). Paragon plans to expand its scope in the future to include mutual funds, futures, commodities, news, and other exchanges.

InterQuote is a software program designed to run from your own computer. It currently comes in several flavors for Unix systems, but will be available in a DOS/Windows version too. This is the major downside about the service from the perspective of the individual user. If you don't have a Unix system, you can access InterQuote via Telnet. Paragon Software even lets you test-drive their system via Telnet: simply log in under the username guest. The basic concept with their program is that you create one or more portfolios of securities. The portfolios report only price-related information—don't

Paragon Software, Inc.

(This page is still under construction.)

Paragon Software is proud to introduce the **InterQuote (sm)** family of stock market services:

1. **Real Time** Market Service
2. **15 Minute Delayed** Market Service
3. **End of Day Market** Service
4. **End of Day Email** Updates

InterQuote provides information on the NYSE, AMEX, NASDAQ, OPRA, and CME exchanges on stocks, options, indices, and mutual funds. The first 3 services allow you to use the InterQuote software on your computer *or ours*, to receive **continuously updating** market information! The email service allows you to receive closing information on your favorite securities at the end of the day.

You can try InterQuote now by telnetting to iq.interquote.com or, simply **by clicking here.**

FOR MORE INFORMATION about InterQuote: Click here or send a blank email message to info@interquote.com. We will also send you a registration form.

Figure 2.29: Look here for information on how to get real-time and delayed quotes over the Internet.

expect to be able to track performance or receive news or price alerts. A portfolio can have up to 200 securities in it. The information provided on securities includes:

◆ Last Price and Volume, Tick Direction

◆ Change and Previous Close

◆ Bid and Ask Prices, and Range on the Day

◆ Today's Open, High, Low, and Volume

◆ 52-Week High and Low Prices

◆ Current P/E Ratio

When setting up a portfolio, you can select which items from this list you want and set the order in which they appear. Paragon has three predefined portfolios: the Dow Jones Industrial, Transportation, and Utilities indexes. Portfolio capabilities vary somewhat between the different types of service. Closing end-of-day quotes via e-mail are free and are included with the other services. You can get prices on one portfolio e-mailed after the market closes each trading day. This will be useful to the many people who do not have full Internet access.

If you have full Internet access, you can get quotes interactively from Paragon. This can be with either real-time, delayed, or closing prices. You can set up a maximum of six portfolios, each containing up to 200 securities. Delayed and real-time services update quotes continuously.

Send an e-mail message to info@paragon.wwa.com to receive its current automated information sheet. If you have more specific questions, send e-mail to support@paragon.wwa.com.

PAWWS—Portfolio Accounting World-Wide from Security APL

http://pawws.secapl.com/

Security APL created and manages this Web page and its services. You can find more background information about this area in the Portfolio Management section of Part Two. The PAWWS Web page has a *Free Services* area that includes a quote server. You can enter a stock symbol and get a delayed quote that includes company name, last price, date and time of last trade, price change, percent change, volume, number of trades, bid and ask prices, high and low of the day, and 52-week high and low prices. This quote server tends to be heavily trafficked during trading hours, so be prepared for slow response times.

QuoteCom

ftp.quote.com

http://www.quote.com/

In this entry I focus on the parts of QuoteCom that provide access to news. (I cover most of QuoteCom's services in the section on Fundamental Stock Analysis earlier in Part Two; I also cover some of its features under the Portfolio Management section.)

The *Basic Service*, which costs $9.95 per month, provides a brief summary of market activity in each of the daily Portfolio Reports sent to a subscriber's e-mail address. Each report also lists the news service(s) and headline(s) for each news item released that day on all companies listed in your portfolio. You can get headlines for news stories that appeared on S&P MarketScope Alerts, BusinessWire, and PR Newswire. To get this information, you will need to use FTP to connect to ftp.quote.com using your login name and password. Go to the directory /pub/updates/news, where you will find daily files going back several months. Each headline has the associated news service and a number. You can use this number to then retrieve the story from QuoteCom's e-mail server.

Wtb QuoteCom's Basic Service, you can get headlines for news stories that appeared on S&P MarketScope Alerts, BusinessWire, and PR Newswire.

For a given day, you can use QuoteCom's Web server to select a specific news service. To see the headlines for the current day's news, select the desired news service icon from the Web page, then select the Submit command. You will be prompted to enter your username and password. QuoteCom will then display a list of the headlines for that day. If you do not subscribe to that news service, you will be charged for each story you retrieve (although it is relatively inexpensive, about one dollar per story).

Telescan

http://www.telescan.com/

I discuss Telescan primarily in the Technical Analysis section earlier in Part Two. Telescan is an online service that is being developed for access via the Internet. This process should be well under way by the time this book reaches the stores. Telescan is a very comprehensive online service that focuses specifically on the area of finance and investing.

One area that is currently functioning under the *Telescan Investment Center* section of the Web page is *Investor Resources*. The first feature is a list of the daily best and worst performers. There are actually four lists: Largest Percent Gainers, Largest Percent Losers, Highest 18-Week Relative Strength, and Lowest 18-Week Relative Strength. The lists include approximately 20 securities each, and provide ticker symbol, name, and either percentage change or relative strength number. I think that the Percent Gainers/Losers lists would be more valuable if they showed the underlying price and its total change on the day, because these lists are frequently dominated by penny stocks. (The arithmetic is simple—a $3 stock that moves $1 has a 33% gain/loss. A $60 per share stock would have to move up or down by more than $20 to appear ahead of the penny stock on either of these lists.) Along this vein, I would also like to see another pair of lists that show those stocks with the largest total dollar gain/loss on the day.

Another feature in the Investor Resources area is the Market Snapshot. Here you can get summary information on several indexes and exchanges, including the closing price and total change on the day for the following indexes:

◆ Dow Jones Composite, Industrials, Transportation, and Utilities

◆ NYSE, AMEX, and NASDAQ Composites

◆ S&P 500 and S&P 100

You can also get some data on the number of advancing, declining, and unchanged securities; total, up, and down volumes; and the TRIN, a technical breadth indicator.

Online Trading

This is a very new area to investing on the Internet. Currently, I know of only two services that offer this type of capability, but I think that you will see many more online trading services become available as two things happen. First, a workable means of providing security and privacy must become established in order for people to feel confident that their investments are safe. Network hacking is an issue that has received much publicity, and, unfortunately, the aspects behind it are complex enough that most people find the issue to be too confusing to understand clearly. Second, the number of online trading services will grow as the current online services such as America Online, CompuServe, and Prodigy provide Internet users with access to their services.

K. Aufhauser & Company

http://www.aufhauser.com/

Aufhauser is a brokerage firm that offers a wide array of services, and now it is making some of them available over the Internet. Several of the services are offered only to clients that have an account with Aufhauser (primarily online order execution); however, some are available to the public, including a 20-minute delayed quote server and several FAQ lists. Figure 2.30 shows the Aufhauser Web site.

The quote server provides delayed price information on equities, options, mutual funds, and indexes. You can enter up to ten ticker symbols, separated by spaces, per update. The server returns closing price, bid and ask prices, high and low prices for the day, and volume. The Web page even has an Option Symbol Guide to help users find the correct strike price and expiration codes. You can actually enter option symbols in either a long or short format, but you must put a hyphen between the security symbol and the expiration/strike letters for the short format (IBM March 80 calls would be IBM-CP, for example).

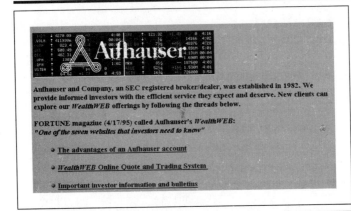

Figure 2.30:
Browse here for information about trading on the Internet.

I did have a problem once getting a correct mutual fund price here. On Sunday, March 12, I entered the mutual fund ticker FLATX, which is the Fidelity Latin America fund had an NAV of $7.92 on Friday, March 10. However, the quote server returned a value of 29¼.

Aufhauser has done an excellent job of preparing a set of FAQ lists that cover aspects pertaining to trading securities, particularly stocks. The lists are more of an explanation about a particular subject than a series of questions and answers. The lists clearly detail several poorly understood aspects of trading, including:

◆ Instinet

◆ SelectNet

◆ Short Selling

◆ NASDAQ Bid/Ask Spreads

Instinet and SelectNet are two means of executing over-the-counter stock orders, short selling refers to the practice of selling units of a security that you do not already own, and NASDAQ bid/ask spreads refer to questions about how the practices of stock trading on the NASDAQ exchange differ from those on the NYSE and AMEX exchanges. You can request an e-mail copy of their FAQs, if you don't have Web access, by sending a message to info@aufhauser.com.

Aufhauser offers online order entry to their clients with a system called *WealthWeb*. There is no minimum deposit required to open an account at Aufhauser. If you have an account with them, you can place orders on stocks, options, and bonds through the Internet. When placing an online order through Aufhauser, you have the ability to specify the following:

Transaction	Contingency	Duration
Buy	Limit	Day order
Sell	Market	GTC (good until canceled)
Sell short	Stop	Stop/limit

After placing an order or orders, you have the ability to check on its status or cancel it if you choose to do so. You can also review your account. To some extent this is the same as generating a current holdings report from a portfolio management program. You can check on your cash balance, equity, buying power, market value, trade balance, settlement balance, and more.

Aufhauser offers several advantages to having an account with them and using their online services. They will provide you with information that they have access to through expensive high-end trading systems, which include:

◆ Bloomberg, Dow Jones, and Reuters News Services

◆ Research Reports and Recommendations

◆ Extensive Securities Database

◆ Instinet and SelectNet

You also get a 10% discount on commissions for placing orders electronically. They describe the following commission schedule:

◆ $34 for the first 1,700 shares, plus $0.02 per share after that

◆ $25 plus $2.50 per option contract (for the first nine), and $2 per contract above that

◆ $39 flat fee per Treasury Bill, Note, or Bond

◆ $5 per bond for U.S. Corporate Bonds

◆ No commission for any foreign bond or bond purchase above $25,000

Net Investor

http://pawws.secapl.com/How_phtml/top.shtml

Howe Barnes Investments, Inc. has teamed up with Security APL to bring online trading to investors through the Internet (see Figure 2.31). Its service is called The Net Investor and provides order-entry capabilities for stocks and mutual funds. You need to open an account with Howe Barnes in order to use Net Investor. You use Security APL's PAWWS portfolio management program, The Source, to enter orders and track investments. (Refer to the Portfolio Management section earlier in Part Two to get more information about The Source and other services available through Security APL.) The Source provides real-time quotes to subscribers of The Net Investor, as opposed to the delayed quotes that are provided to regular Source users.

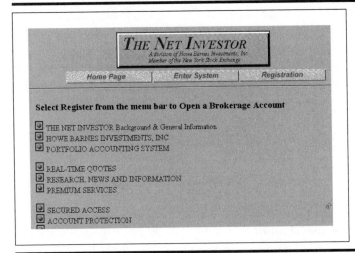

Figure 2.31:
Here is another site where you can trade over the Internet.

You must deposit a minimum of $2,000 to open an account with Howe Barnes and use The Net Investor. The current commission schedules for online trades of stocks and mutual funds are listed in Tables 2.8 and 2.9 respectively.

Stocks priced less than $1 have a different commission schedule.

Table 2.8: The Net Investor Commission Schedule for Stocks

Dollar Amount	Regular Fee	Frequent Trader's Fee
Less than $2,500	$ 38	$ 35
$2,501 to $5,000	$ 48	$ 43
$5,001 to $10,000	$ 68	$ 58
$10,001 to $25,000	$ 95	$ 76
$25,001 to $50,000	$125	$100
$50,001 and higher	$100 + 0.1% of amount invested	25% discount on the regular fee

Table 2.9: The Net Investor Commission Schedule for Mutual Funds

Amount	Commission
Less than $5,000	$40
$5,001 to $10,000	$50
$10,001 to 15,000	$60
$15,001 to $25,000	$70
More than $25,000	$45 + 0.1% of amount invested

Appendices

A: Where Do I Go
   from Here?

B: Internet Service
   Providers

Where Do I Go from Here?

Now that you know the basics and what's out there on the Internet, you may want to find out more. For example, you may want to learn in more detail about the World Wide Web, Usenet, Gopher, and FTP, *and* the software and tools you can use to make the most of your Internet travels.

If you'd like a basic, plain-English tour of the Internet and its uses, then *A Guided Tour of the Internet* by Christian Crumlish is for you. It's like having an Internet guru at your side, explaining everything as you go along. Another great book for newbies is *Access the Internet* by David Peal. This book even includes NetCruiser software, which will get you connected via an easy point-and-click interface in no time.

For an introduction to the World Wide Web, turn to *Mosaic Access to the Internet* or *Surfing the Internet with Netscape*, both by Daniel A. Tauber and Brenda Kienan. Each of these books walks you through getting connected, and they both include the software you need to get started on the Web in a jiffy.

For quick and easy Internet reference, turn to the *Internet Instant Reference* by Paul Hoffman, and for an in-depth overview, try the best-selling *Internet Roadmap* by Bennett Falk. To get familiar with the lingo, you can turn to the compact and concise *Internet Dictionary* by Christian Crumlish.

If you've just got to learn *all* there is to know about the Internet, the comprehensive, complete *Mastering the Internet* by Glee Harrah Cady and Pat McGregor is for you. And if you want to find out what tools and utilities are available (including a wealth of tools available on the Internet itself) to maximize the power of your Internet experience, you'll want to check out *The Internet Tool Kit* by Nancy Cedeno.

All of these books have been published by Sybex in 1995 editions.

Internet Service Providers

If you need to set up an account with an Internet service provider, this is the place for you. This appendix lists providers in the United States, Canada, Great Britain, Ireland, Australia, and New Zealand.

The service providers listed here offer full Internet service, including SLIP/PPP accounts, which allow you to use Web browsers like Mosaic and Netscape.

The list we're providing here is by no means comprehensive. We're concentrating on service providers that offer national or nearly national Internet service in English-speaking countries. You may prefer to go with a service provider that's local to your area. (To minimize your phone bill, it is important to find a service provider that offers a local or toll-free phone number for access.)

What's Out There

Two very good sources of information about Internet service providers are available on the Internet itself. Peter Kaminski's Public Dialup Internet Access List (PDIAL) is located at ftp://ftp.net-com.com/pub/in/info-deli/public-access/pdial. Yahoo's Internet Access Providers list is at http://www.yahoo.com/Business/Corporations/Internet_Access_providers/.

When you inquire into establishing an account with any of the providers listed in this appendix, tell them the type of account you want—you may want a "shell account" if you know and plan to use Unix commands to get around, or you may want the type of point-and-click access that's offered through a graphical interface. If you want to run a Web browser like Mosaic or Netscape, you must have a SLIP or PPP account. Selecting an Internet service provider is a matter of personal preference and local access. Shop around, and if you aren't satisfied at any point, change providers.

When you're shopping around for an Internet service provider, the most important questions to ask are (a) What is the nearest local access number? (b) What are the monthly service charges? and (c) Is there a setup (or registration) fee?

IN THE UNITED STATES

In this section we list Internet service providers that provide local-access phone numbers in most major American cities. These are the big, national companies. Many areas also have smaller, regional Internet providers, which may offer better local access if you're not in a big city. You can find out about these smaller companies by looking in local computer papers like *MicroTimes* or *Computer Currents* or by getting on the Internet via one of these big companies and checking out the Peter Kaminski and Yahoo service provider listings.

Opening an account with any of the providers listed here will get you full access to the World Wide Web, and full-fledged e-mail service (allowing you to send and receive e-mail). You'll also get the ability to read and post articles to Usenet newsgroups.

Netcom Netcom Online Communications Services is a national Internet service provider with local access numbers in most major cities. (As of this writing, they have 100 local access numbers in the United States.) Netcom's NetCruiser software gives you a point-and-click graphical interface to the Internet. (Netcom also provides a shell account, but stay away from it if you want to run Netscape.) Starting with NetCruiser version 1.6, it is possible to run Netscape on top of NetCruiser. Especially for beginning users who want a point-and-click interface and easy setup of Netscape, this may be a good choice.

NetCruiser software is available on disk for free but without documentation at many trade shows and bookstores. It is also available with a very good book (*Access the Internet, Second Edition*; David Peal, Sybex, 1995) that shows you how to use the software. To contact Netcom directly, phone (800) 353-6600.

Performance Systems International Performance Systems International is a national Internet Service Provider with local access numbers in many American cities *and in Japan*. These folks are currently upgrading their modems to 28.8 Kilobits per second, which will give you faster access to the Internet.

To contact PSI directly, phone (800) 82P-SI82.

UUNet/AlterNet UUNet Technologies and AlterNet offer Internet service throughout the United States. They run their own national network.

You can contact UUnet and AlterNet at (800) 488-6383.

Portal Portal Communications, Inc., an Internet Service Provider located in the San Francisco Bay Area, lets you get connected either by dialing one of their San Francisco Bay Area phone numbers or via the CompuServe network. (This is not CompuServe Information Services, but rather the network on which CompuServe runs.) The CompuServe network, with over 400 access numbers, is a local call from most populous cities in the United States.

You can contact Portal at (408) 973-9111.

IN CANADA

Listed here are providers that offer access to Internet service in the areas around large Canadian cities. For information about local access in less populated regions, get connected and check out the Peter Kaminski and Yahoo lists described earlier in this appendix.

Many Internet service providers in the U.S. also offer service in Canada and in border towns near Canada. If you're interested and you're in Canada, you can ask some of the big American service providers whether they have a local number near you.

UUNet Canada UUNet Canada is the Canadian division of the United States service provider UUNet/AlterNet, which we described earlier in this chapter. UUNet Canada offers Internet service to large portions of Canada.

You can contact UUNet Canada directly by phoning (416) 368-6621.

Internet Direct Internet Direct offers access to folks in the Toronto and Vancouver areas.

You can contact Internet Direct by phoning (604) 691-1600 or faxing (604) 691-1605.

IN GREAT BRITAIN AND IRELAND

The Internet is international. Here are some service providers located and offering service in Great Britain and Ireland.

UNet Located in the northwest part of England, with more locations promised, UNet offers access at speeds up to 28.8 Kilobits per second along with various Internet tools for your use.

They can be reached by phone at 0925 633 144.

Easynet London-based Easynet provides Internet service throughout England via Pipex, along with a host of Internet tools.

You can reach them by phone at 0171 209 0990.

Ireland On-Line Serving most (if not all) of Ireland, including Belfast, Ireland On-Line offers complete Internet service including ISDN and leased-line connections.

Contact Ireland On-Line by phone at 00 353 (0)1 8551740.

IN AUSTRALIA AND NEW ZEALAND

Down under in Australia and New Zealand, the Internet is as happening as it is in the northern hemisphere; many terrific sites are located in Australia especially. Here are a couple of service providers for that part of the world.

Connect.com.au In wild and woolly Australia, Internet service (SLIP/PPP) is available from Connect.com.au Pty Ltd.

You can contact the people at Connect.com.au by phone at 61 3 528 2239.

Actrix Actrix Information Exchange offers Internet service (PPP accounts) in the Wellington, New Zealand area.

You can reach these folks by phone at 64 4 389 6316.

Index

Note to the Reader: Throughout this index **boldfaced** page numbers indicate primary discussions of a topic. *Italicized* page numbers indicate illustrations.

162

The Complete Pocket Tour Series from Sybex

A Pocket Tour of:

Games on the Internet

Health & Fitness on the Internet

Money on the Internet

Music on the Internet

Sports on the Internet

Travel on the Internet

with more coming soon to a store near you.